WORKING PAPERS

DUPREE

VOLUME I CHAPTERS 1-12
to accompany

PRINCIPLES OF ACCOUNTING

DUPREE • MARDER

ADDISON-WESLEY PUBLISHING COMPANY

Reading, Massachusetts • Menlo Park, California • London
Amsterdam • Don Mills, Ontario • Sydney

To the Student

This volume provides working papers for use in solving self-quizzes and problems in Chapters 1 through 12 of *Principles of Accounting* by Dempsey Dupree and Matthew Marder. Where appropriate, selected information is already preprinted on the forms. Solutions to problems and alternate problems generally fit on the same forms. For the few exceptions, additional forms are provided. All oversized forms are located at the back of this volume.

ISBN 0-201-11382-1
DEFGHIJ-AL-89876

Name ____________________

Section __________ Date __________

1. a.

b.

c.

2. a.

b.

c.

d.

e.

f.

g.

3. a.

b.

3. c.

d.

Name ______________________

Section ______________ Date ____________

1. Assets = Liability + Owners Equity

2. Assets = Liabilities + Owner's Equity

Cash	+	Office Supplies	+	Car	=	Note Payable	+	R. Flox, Capital

a) $3,000 =
b) 20 Asset
c) 500 Asset 5,000 notes payable
d) 400 cash withdrawn
e) 200 payment on notes payable

2,600 + 20 + 5500 = 4,800 + 3320

3.

FLOX COMPANY
Balance Sheet
September 30, 19--

Assets		Liabilities	
Cash	$4000 —	Notes Payable	$4200 —
Accounts Receivable	75 —	Owners Equity	
Car	5500 —	R. Flox Capital	5375 —
Total Assets	9575 —	Total Liabilities and Owner's Equity	9575 —

4. Assets = Liabilities + Owner's Equity

Cash	+	Accounts Receivable	+	Gasoline	=	Accounts Payable	+	J. Ripe, Capital
1,000	+	500	+	280	=	330	+	1,450

a) $250 Jan. rent
b) +90 Electric Bill pd in Feb
c) $50 Gasoline
d) +$400 cash for services
e) +$600 Accounts Receivable

cash + Acc Rec + Gasoline = Acc Pay. + J. Ripe. Capital
1150 + 1100 + 230 = 420 + 2,060

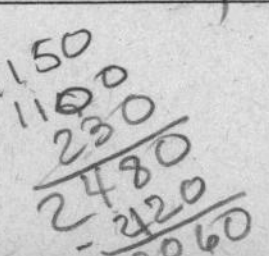

5.

ACORN TREE SERVICE
Income Statement
For the Month of January, 19--

Service Revenue		$2000 —
Expenses		
Wage expense	$500 —	
Depr. expense	150 —	
Gasoline expense	200 —	
Rent expense	400 —	1250 —
Net income		$750 —

6. a. entity - seperating business expenses from personal expences

b. Monetary is money

c. Cost - is what you pay for something

d. realization - recognized revenue at the point of sale

e. Matching is when the expenditures match the time they were supposed to be used

f. A time period can be a Fiscal year or From Jan 1 to Dec 31 or what ever time a statement wishes to cover

1.B.1. $88,600 = $36,800 + $51,800

1.B.2. a. 120,000 = 70,000 + 50,000
b. 60,000 = 25,000 + 35,000
c 62,000 = 30,400 + 31,600
d 28,700 = 17,800 + 10,900

1.B.3. a. 250,000 - 198,000 = 52,000
b. 86,000 - 76,200 = 9,800
c. 178,000 - 150,000 = 28,000
d. 94,000 - 110,000 = (16,000)

1.B4. a. F c. T e. F g. T
b. F d. F f. T h. T or F

Name Donna Hanna

Section ________ Date 1/26/87

PROBLEM 1.B.5. & ALTERNATE

Rigby Company
Balance Sheet
December 31, 19—

Assets		Liabilities	
Cash	$800 —	Note payable	$3600 —
Supplies	75 —		
Calculator	420 —		
Automobile	6100 —	Owners Equity	
		Rigby, Capital	3795 —
Total Assets	$7395 —	Total Liabilities & Owners' Equity	$7395 —

Belwah Company
Balance Sheet
December 31, 19--

Assets		Liabilities	
Fees Earned	$4,200—	Wage expense	$3,600—
		Rent expense	500—
		Supplies expense	200—
		Tel. & utilities exp.	180—
		Entertainment exp.	250—
		Total Liabilities	4,730—
		Owners Equity	
		Belwah Company, Capital	(530—)
Total Assets	$4,200—	Total Liab & Own equity	$4,200—

Name ______________________

Section __________ Date __________

PROBLEM 1.B.6. & ALTERNATE

Belwah Company

Income Statement

December 31, 19--

Fees earned		$4200 —
Expenses		
Wage expense	$3600 —	
Rent expense	500 —	
Supplies expense	200 —	
Telephone and utilities expense	180 —	
Entertainment expense	250 —	4730 —
Net Loss		($ 530 —)

Name ________________________ PROBLEM 1.B.7

Section ____________ Date ____________

a)

ZAP COMPANY
Balance Sheet
July 1, 19--

Assets		Liabilities	
Cash	$7000—		—
		Owners Equity	
		U. Zap, Capital	$7000—
Total Assets	$7000—	Total Liabilities + Owners Equity	7000—

b)

ZAP COMPANY
Balance Sheet
July 5, 19--

Assets		Liabilities	
Land	$10000—	Notes Payable	$6000—
Cash	3000—	Owners Equity	
		U. Zap, Capital	$7000—
Total Assets	$13000—		$13000—

c)

ZAP COMPANY
Balance Sheet
July 7, 19--

Assets		Liabilities	
Land	$10000—	Notes Payable	$6000—
Cash	2400—	Owners Equity	
Tools	600—	U. Zap, Capital	7000—
Total Assets	$13000—	Total Liabilities + Owners Equity	$13000—

Name ______________________________ PROBLEM 1.B.8.

Section ______________ Date ____________

ALEX GANDER COMPANY
Income Statement
For the Month Ended April 30, 19--

Fees earned		$ 3300 —
Rent revenue		450 —
		3750 —
Wage expense	$ 1100 —	
Utilities expense	125 —	
Rent expense	900 —	
Other expense	180 —	2305 —
Net Income		$ 1445 —

or

Revenues		
Fees earned		$ 3300 —
Rent Revenue		450 —
		3750 —
Expenses		
Wage expense	$ 1100 —	
Utilities expense	125 —	
Rent expense	900 —	
Other expense	180 —	2305 —
Net Income		$1445 —

12,350
150
500
12,000
25,000

15,000
2,650
12,350

12,350
150
500
12,000
250,00

2,000
500
150
2650

Name ____________________

Section __________ Date __________

PROBLEM 1.B.9

1) a) +15,000 Cash
+15,000 OE

b) -150 Cash
+150 OFFICE SUPPLIES

c) -500 Cash
+500 Typewriter

d) -2,000 Cash
+12,000 Truck
+10,000 Accts Payable

2) Assets = Liabilities + Owner's Equity

	Cash	+	Office Supplies	+	Typewriter	+	Truck	=	Note Payable	+	O. Bundy, Capital
a)	15,000							=			15,000
b)	-150		+150					=			
c)	-500				+500						
d)	-2,000						+12,000	=	+10,000		
Column Totals	12,350	+	150	+	500	+	12,000	=	10,000		15,000

3)

BUNDY COMPANY
Balance Sheet
June 3, 19--

Assets		Liabilities	
Cash	$12350 —	Notes Payable	$10000 —
Supplies	150 —		
Typewriter	500 —	Owners Equity	
Truck	12000 —	Bundy Company Capital	15000 —
Total Assets	$25000 —	Total Liabilities + Owners Equity	$25000 —

3,000
50
800
3,850
-500
3350

Name ____________________

Section ____________ Date ____________

PROBLEM 1.B.10.

SOHO COMPANY

	Assets					=	Liabilities	+	Owner's Equity
	Cash	+	Office Supplies	+	Accounts Receivable	=	Accounts Payable	+	B. Soho, Capital
1)	3,000	+	50	+	800	=	500	+	3,5000

2) a) −1,500 Cash

b) +120 Accounts Payable

c) −18 Supplies

d) +25 Accounts Payable

e) +100 Cash; −100 Accounts Receivable

f) +2500 Cash

g) −30 Cash

410
140
270

5,990
1,500
410
6,000
13,900
2,200
16,100

12,750
− 270
12,480

Name ____________________

Section __________ Date __________

		Assets				=	Liabilities	+	Owner's Equity
		Cash	+ Accounts Receivable	+ Advertising Supplies	+ Office Equipment	=	Accounts Payable	+	Capital
1)	a)	10,000				=	—	+	10,000
	b)	10,000			6,000	=	6,000	+	10,000
	c)	9,590		+ 410	+ 6,000	=	6,000	+	10,000
	d)	9,590	+ 500	+ 410	+ 6,000	=	6,000	+	10,500
	e)	8,990	+ 500	+ 410	+ 6,000	=	6,000	+	9,900
	f)	5,990	+ 500	+ 410	+ 6,000	=	3,000	+	9,900
	g)	5,990	+ 2,700	+ 410	+ 6,000	=	3,000	+	12,100
	h)	6,490	+ 2,200	+ 410	+ 6,000	=	3,000	+	12,100
	i)	5,490	+ 2,200	+ 410	+ 6,000	=	3,000	+	11,100
	j)	5,490	+ 2,200	+ 410	+ 6,000	=	3,150	+	10,950
	k)	5,490	+ 3,000	+ 410	+ 6,000	=	3,150	+	11,750
	l)	5,490	+ 3,000	+ 140	+ 6,000	=	3,150	+	11,480
	Adj.								

2)

5,490	3,150
3,000	11,480
140	14,630
6,000	
14,630	

3)

Gruner Ad Agency

Income Statement

March 31, 19--

4)

Balance Sheet

5) This is the realization concept even though it will be received later it is counted as being earned now.

6)

Name ______________________

Section ____________ Date ____________

PROBLEM 1.2. & ALTERNATE

		Assets								=	Liabilities	+	Owner's Equity
		Cash	+	Accounts Receivable	+	Office Supplies	+	Calculator	+	Furniture	=	Accounts Payable	+	Capital
1)	a)													
	b)													
	c)													
	d)													
	e)													
	f)													
	g)													
	h)													
	i)													
	j)													
	k)													
	Adj.													

2)

Income Statement

3)

Balance Sheet

4)

5)

Name ______________________

Section ____________ Date ____________

COMPREHENSION PROBLEM 1.3.

1)

SHUSTER REFUSE COMPANY
Income Statement
For the Year Ended December 31, 19X4

2)

SHUSTER REFUSE COMPANY
Balance Sheet
December 31, 19X4

3)

SHUSTER REFUSE COMPANY
Balance Sheet
December 31, 19X3

4)

Name ____________________

Section ____________ Date ____________

1. Debit means right.
Credit means left.

2. T accounts are abbreviated versions of ledger accounts
T accounts on the left side of the equation ar debited
on the left side and T accounts on the right side
of an equation are debited on the right side.

3.

Cash

Debit	Credit
20,000	5,000
500	2,000

Truck

Debit	Credit
12,500	

Note Payable

Debit	Credit
	12,000

Wage Expense

Debit	Credit
2,000	

Delivery Fees

Debit	Credit
500	

I. M. Worthy, Capital

Debit	Credit
	20,000

4. A. Proprietorship – a business owned by one person

B. Partnership – a business owned by two or more people

C. Corporation – An association in which ownership is represented by shares of stock.

2A1. a. right.
b. decrease
c. debits
d. credits

2A2. a. True; False Even if there is a note payable the assets are increased.
b. True; On the right side of an equation the left side is decrease and the right side is increase
c. True; A debit on the right side of an equation means a decrease
d. False; It would affect the cash account + the truck account on the asset side.
e. True; A debit on the left side of an equation is an increase
f. False; A debit on the right side would mean a decrease
g. True; A decrease of an asset account would be a credit

2A.3. 1/1; M. Blaine put 90,000 into business
1/3; land was purchased for 10,000 for cash
1/4; Purchased a building for 30,000; 15,000 cash + 15,000 on credit
1/10; Purchased taxicabs for 40,000 cash
1/12; Purchased uniforms for 400 on account
1/16; Paid $2,000 on mortgage payable
1/17; Borrowed 20,000
1/21; Purchased Taxicabs for 40,000; 30,000 cash + 10,000 on account
1/27; Purchased taxicabs on credit for 20,000

2.A.4. a. (1) Cash is an asset; increased; debited
E. Grazio is OE; decreased; credited
b. (1) Building account; asset; increased; debited / Cash account; asset; decreased; credited / Notes payable; liability, increased; credited
c. cash; asset; decreased; credited
Accounts payable; liability; decreased; debited
d. cash; asset; decreased; credited
insurance expense; O.E.; decreased, debited
e. Cash; asset; decreased; credited
E Grazio Withdrawal acct.; OE; decreased; debited

Name ______________________

Section ______________ Date ______________

PROBLEM 2.A.5. & ALTERNATE

1)

Cash | Accounts Receivable

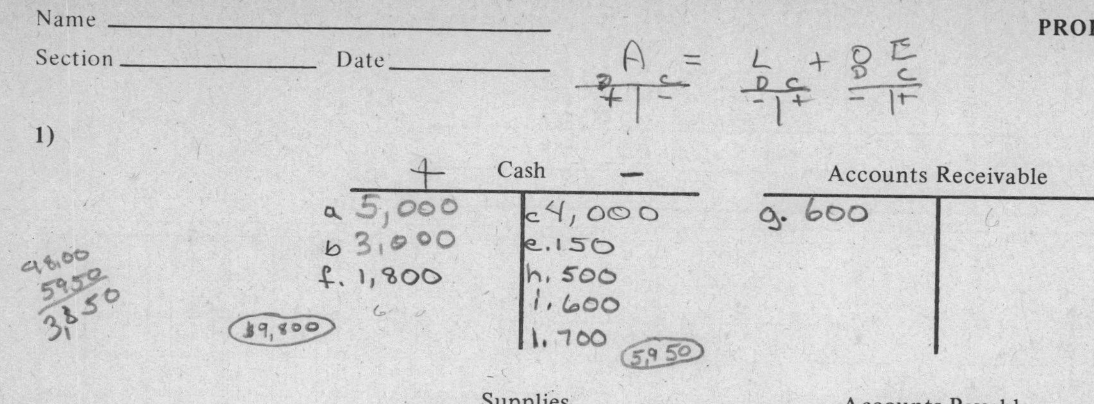

Supplies

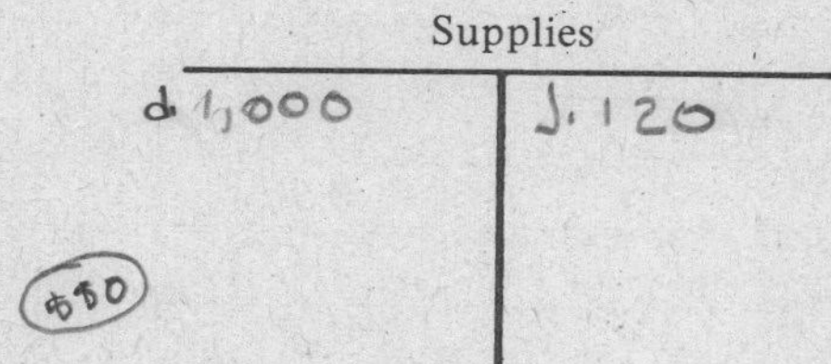

Accounts Payable

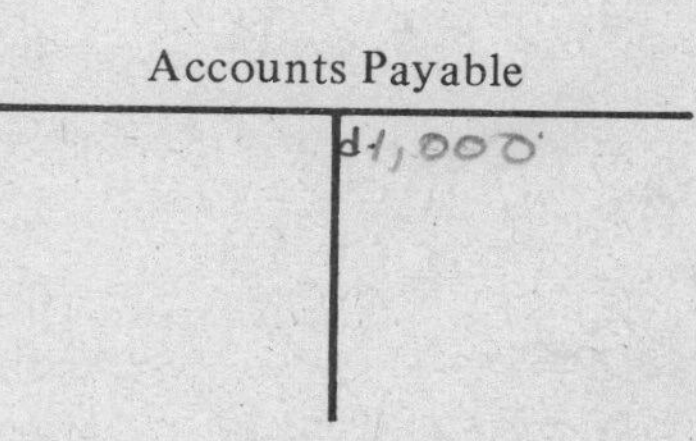

Equipment

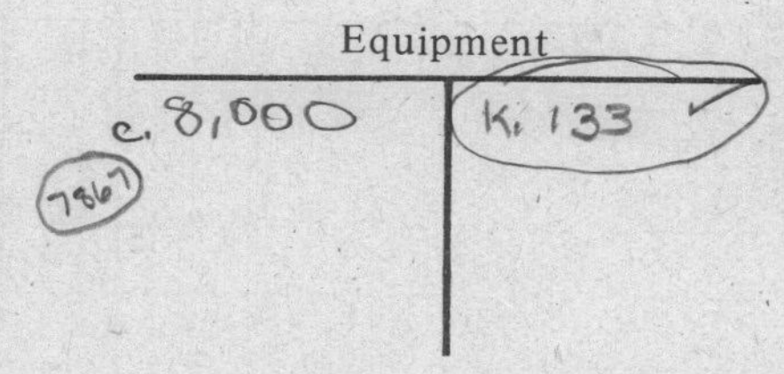

Notes Payable

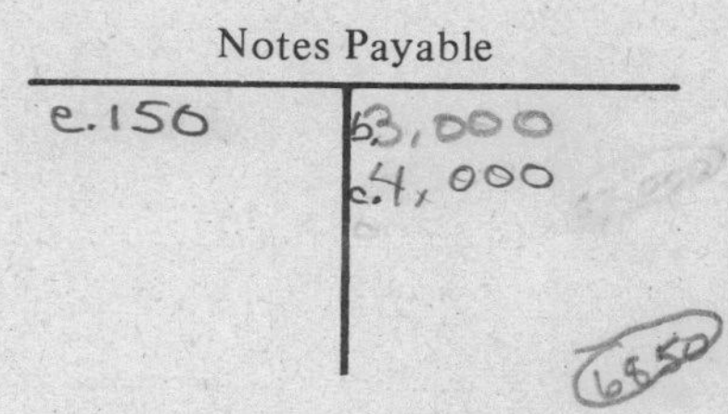

Accum. Depr. – Equip.

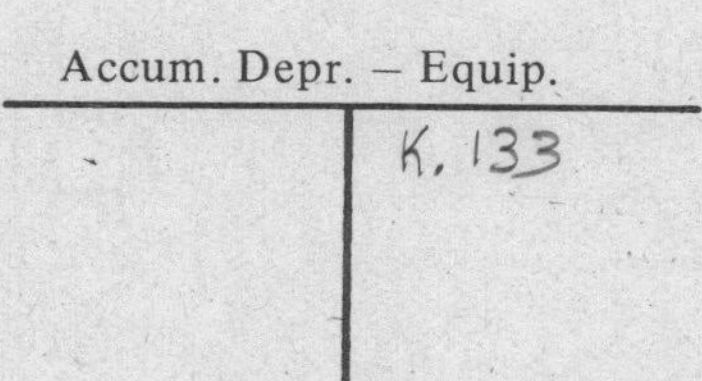

, Capital

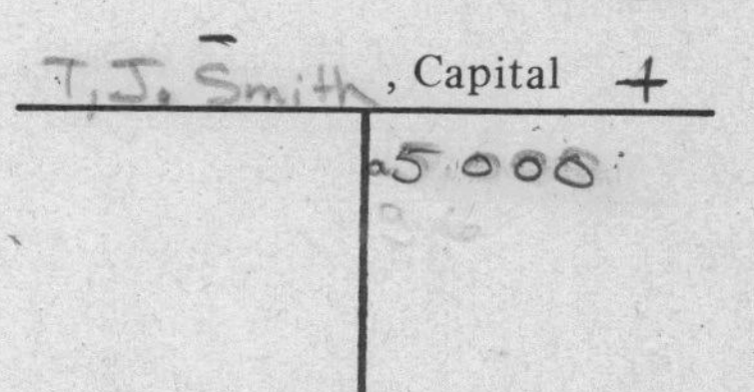

Wage Expense

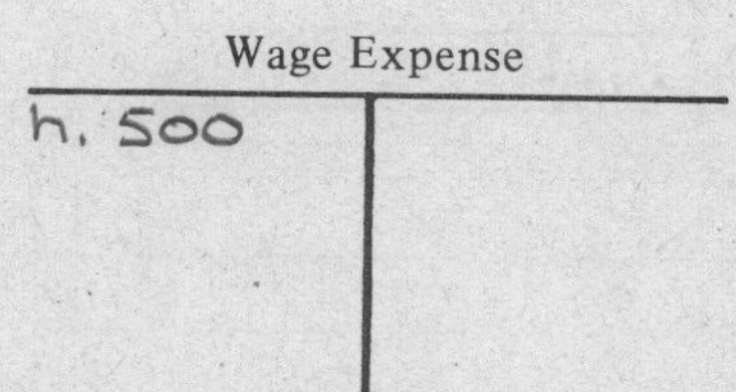

, Withdrawals

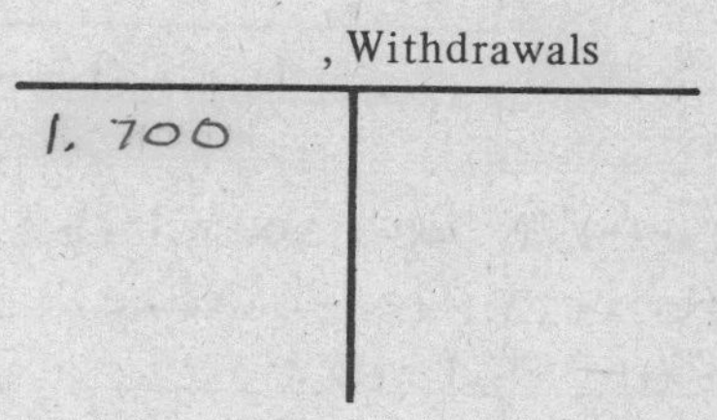

Rent Expense

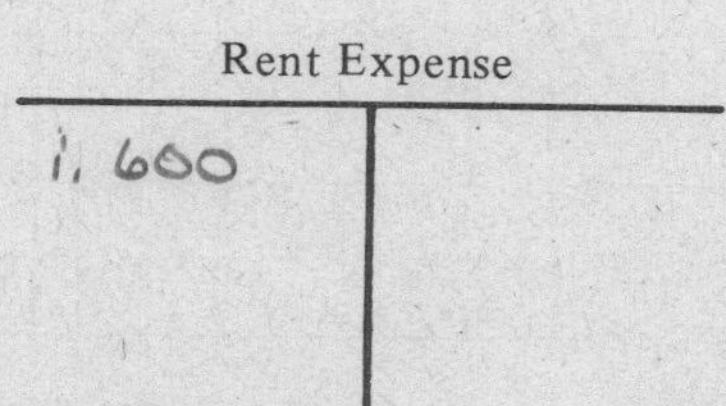

Revenue

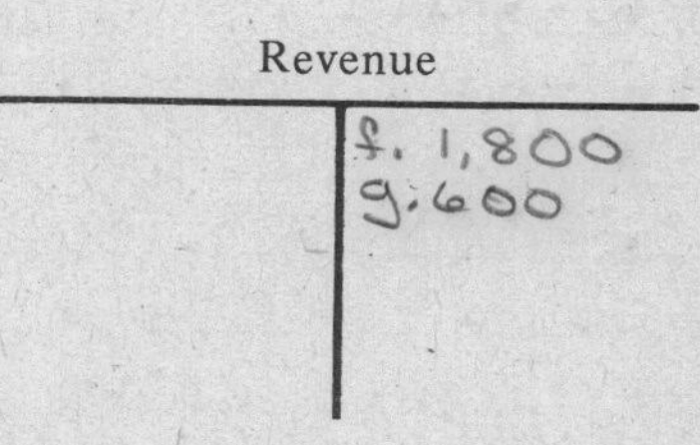

Depreciation Expense | Supplies Expense

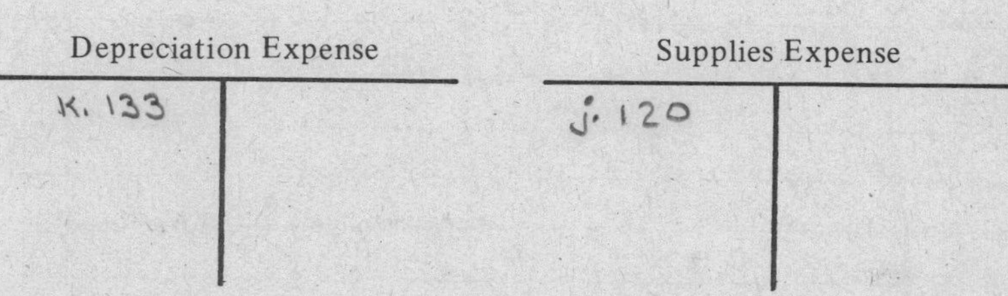

2)

T.J. Smith
Income Statement
October 31, 19--

Revenues		
Cash collected		$ 1800 —
Revenue earned		600 —
		2400 —
Expenses		
Wage expense	$ 500 —	
Rent expense	600 —	
Supplies expense	120 —	
Depreciation expense	133 —	1353 —
Net income		$ 1047

3)

T.J. Smith
Statement of Owner's Capital
October 31, 19--

~~TJ Smith capital, October 1~~		~~$ -0-~~
Owner investment in October		$ 5000 —
Net income for October	$ 1047 —	
Less Owner's withdrawals	700 —	347 —
T.J. Smith, capital, October 31		$ 5347 —

Name ______________________

Section ____________ Date ________

4)

T.J. Smith

Balance Sheet

October 31, 19--

Assets		$ 3850—	Liabilities		
Cash		600—	Accounts Payable		$ 1000—
Accounts Receivable		880—	Notes Payable		6850—
Supplies			Total Liabilities		7850—
Equipment	$ 8000—		Owner's Equity		
Less: Accumulated depreciation	133—	7867—	T.J. Smith, Capital		5347—
Total Assets		$ 13197—	Total Liabilities and Owner's Equity		$ 13197—

(1)

Supplies	
100	

Accts. Payable	
	100

(2)

Cash	
	200

Rent Expense	
200	

(3)

Cash	
50	

Revenue	
	50

(4)

Cash	
	100

Accts. Payable	
100	

Name ____________________
Section __________ Date __________

PROBLEM 2.A.6. & ALTERNATE

1)

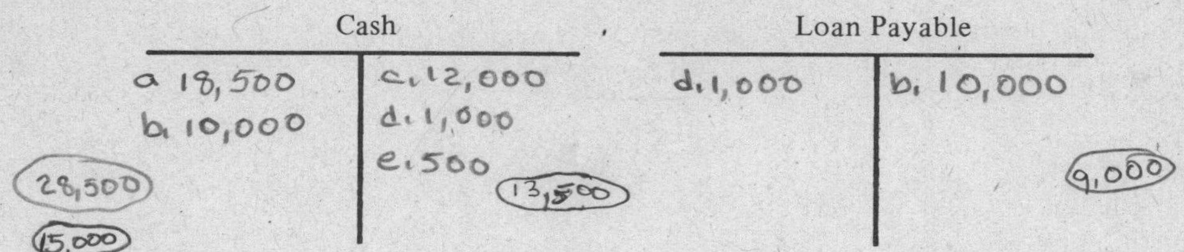

9,000
20
9,020
18,000
27,020

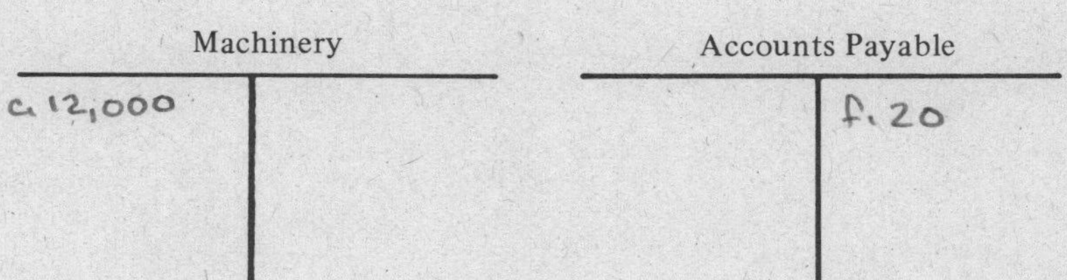

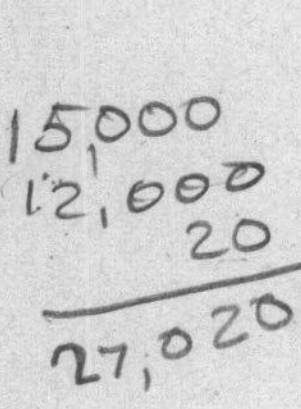

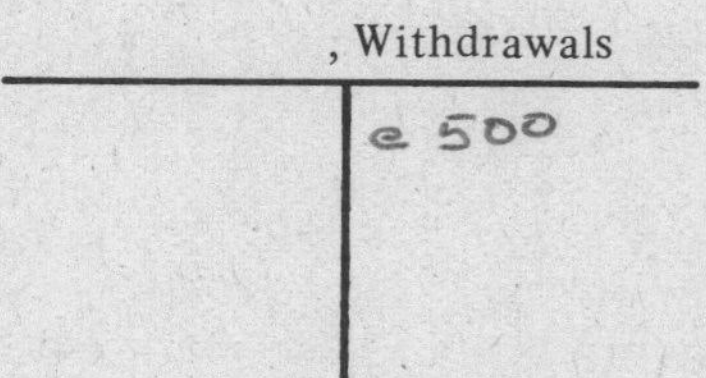

18,000
9,020
27,020

2)

Assets	=	Liabilities	+	Owner's Equity
27,020	=	9,020	+	18,000

Name ______________________ **PROBLEM 2.A.7. & ALTERNATE**

Section ____________ Date ____________

1)

O'Connor Company

Income Statement

June 30, 19--

Revenues		
1st Revenue		$ 3000 —
2nd Revenue		6000 —
		9000 —
Expenses		
Supplies expense	$ 75 —	
Insurance expense	1250 —	
Depreciation expense	100 —	
Rent expense	1200 —	
Wage expense	2500 —	5125 —
Net income		$ 3875 —

10,000 − 8,450 = 1,550

13,675 − 9,800 = 3,875; 3,875 + 6,000 = 9,875

2)

O'Connor Company
Balance Sheet
June 30, 19—

Assets			Liabilities		
Cash		$ 1550—	Accounts Payable		$ 200—
Accounts Receivable		6000—	Notes Payable		3600—
Office Supplies		225—	Total liabilities		3800—
Equipment	$ 6000—		Owners Equity		
Less Accum. Depr.	100—	5900—	J. O'Connor, Capital		9875—
Total Assets		$ 13675—	Total Liabilities + Owners Equity		$ 13675—

Name ______________________ PROBLEM 2.A.8. & ALTERNATE

Section ____________ Date ____________

1) a) cash debited - 10,000
J. Marsh, capital credited - 10,000

b) land, debited 10,000
Building, debited 20,000
cash, credited 6,000
Mortgage payable, credited 24,000

c) Equipment, debited, 3,000
Accounts payable, credited, 3,000

d) Cash, credited, 60
Office supplies, debited 60

e) Cash, credited, 1000
Accounts payable, debited, 1,000

f) Cash, debited, 6,000
Notes payable, credited, 6,000

g) land, debited, 4,000
Cash, credited, 4,000

h) paper bags, wrappers, cups
Supplies, debited, 500
Cash, credited, 500

i) Equipment, debited, 1000
J. Marsh capital, credited 1,000

2)

16,000
11,560
4,440

Cash

a. 10,000	b. 6,000
f. 6,000	d. 60
	e. 1,000
	g. 4,000
	h. 500

Mortgage Payable

	b. 24,000

Land

b. 10,000	
g. 4,000	

Accounts Payable

e. 1,000	c. 3,000

Building

b. 20,000	

Notes Payable

	f. 6,000

Equipment

c. 3,000	
i. 1,000	

Paper bags, wrappers, cups

h. 500	

Office Supplies

d. 60	

J. Marsh, Capital

	a. 10,000
	i. 1,000

3) Roadside Hot Dogs

Cash	$ 4440 —
Land	14000 —
Building	20000 —
Equipment	4000 —
Office Supplies	60 —
Paper bags, Wrappers, cups	500 —
Mortgage Payable	24000 —
Accounts Payable	2000 —
Notes Payable	6000 —
J. Marsh, Capital	11000 —

4)

Roadside Hot dogs
Balance Sheet
April 30, 19--

Assets		Liabilities	
Cash	4440 —	Mortgage Payable	$ 24000 —
Land	14000 —	Accounts Payable	2000 —
Building	20000 —	Notes Payable	6000 —
Equipment	4000 —	Owners Equity	
Office supplies	60 —	J. Marsh, Capital	11000 —
Paper bags, wrappers, cups	500 —	Total Liabilities and	
Total Assets	$ 43000 —	Owner's Equity	$ 43000 —

Name ______________________ **PROBLEM 2.A.9.**

Section ____________ Date ____________

1)

DUNLAP COMPANY
Income Statement
For the Month of May, 19--

Revenues		
Service Revenue a		$ 2700 —
Service Revenue h		1200 —
Expenses		3900 —
Wage Expense	$ 1400 —	
Gasoline Expense	600 —	
Supplies Expense	200 —	
Depreciation Expense	300 —	2500 —
Net income		$ 1400 —

2)

DUNLAP COMPANY
Statement of Owner's Capital
For the Month of May, 19--

A. Dunlap, Capital May 1		$ 2000 —
Owner investment in May		-0-
Net income for May	$ 1400 —	
Less Owner's withdrawals	800 —	600 —
A. Dunlap, Capital May 3-		$ 2600 —

3)

DUNLAP COMPANY
Balance Sheet
May 31, 19--

Assets			Liabilities		
Cash		$ 1600 —	Accounts Payable		$ 600 —
Accounts Receivable		1300 —	Notes Payable		3800 —
Supplies		100 —	Owners Equity		
Truck	$ 8000 —		A. Dunlop Capital		4100 —
Less Depr. - Truck	3300 —	4700 —			
Total Assets		$ 7700 —	Total Liabilities and Owner's Equity		8500 —

Name

Section Date

1. Documenting - The noting of transactions by an entity on business forms.
Recording - Information documented in a journal by date, in chronological order
Summarizing - classifying information into account categories
Reporting - Providing information to people who need it

2. a. Source documents are used in documenting. They can be receipts, invoices, checks, etc.

b. Journals are used in recording. It is the place where an entry is first originally entered.

c. Ledgers are used in summarizing. They are a group of accounts

d. Statements are used in Reporting. A statement is the way Accounting data is formally presented

3. General Journal *PAGE* J1

Date		Account Names and Explanations	A/C #	Debit	Credit
19--					
May	2	Cash	101	1800 --	
		Pam Pence, Capital	301		1800 —
		Deposit No. 1			
	3	Sanding Machine		2000 --	
		Cash	101		500 --
		Notes Payable			1500 --
		Check No. 101			
	4.	Supplies		700 --	
		Accounts Payable			700 --
		Gritty Company			
	15	Cash	101	900 --	
		Revenue			900 --
		Deposit No. 2			
	15	Pam Pence, withdrawal		100 --	
		Cash	101		100 --
		Check No. 102			
	25	Rent Expense		300 --	
		Cash	101		300 --
		Check no. 103			
	25	Accounts Payable		200 --	
		Cash	101		200 --
		Check no. 104			
	31	Wage expense		600 --	
		Cash	101		600 --
		Check no. 105			
	31	Accounts Receivable		1300 --	
		Revenue			1300 --
		Work done / will pay in June			
	31	Sanding machine expense		80 --	
		Sanding machine			80 --
		Depreciation			
	31	Supplies expense		150 --	
		Supplies			150 --
		Used during May			

Name ______________________

Section __________ Date __________

4. Cash ACCOUNT NO. 101

Date		Item	Ref.	Debit	Credit	Balance Debit	Balance Credit
19--							
May	2		J1	1800--		1800--	
	3		J1		500--	1300--	
	15		J1	900--		2200--	
	15		J1		100--	2100--	
	25		J1		300--	1800--	
	25		J1		200--	1600--	
	31		J1		600--	1000--	

Pam Pence, Capital ACCOUNT NO. 301

Date		Item	Ref.	Debit	Credit	Balance Debit	Balance Credit
19--							
May	2		J1		1800--		1800--

cash A + Dr.
Capital OE + Cr.

Cash: 10,000 (debit)
Sidney: 10,000 (credit)

Tools A Debit
Tally Company Payable L + Credit

Tools: 800 (debit)
Tally Co. Payable: 800 (credit)

2, Truck A + debit
cash A − credit
Notes payable L + Credit

Truck: 10,000 (debit)
Cash: 2,000 (credit)
N/P: 8,000 (credit)

cash A − credit
5 Torgue OE − debit

Cash: 200 (credit)
Torgue Withdrawal: 200 (debit)

15 Cash: 800 (credit)
Acc Payable: 800 (debit)

15

Name ______________________ **PROBLEM 2.B.5. & ALTERNATE**

Section ____________ Date ____________

1) **General Journal** *PAGE* J1

Date		Account Names and Explanations	A/C #	Debit	Credit
19--					
Aug.	1	Cash	110	10000 —	
		S. Torgue, Capital	310		10000 —
		Deposit no. 1			
	1	Tools	120	800 —	
		Accounts Payable	210		800 —
		Tally Company			
	2	Truck	130	10000 —	
		Cash	110		2000 —
		Notes Payable	220		8000 —
		Check no. 1			
	5	Torgue Capital, Withdrawal	320	200 —	
		Cash	110		200 —
		Check no. 2			
	15	Accounts Payable	210	800 —	
		Cash	110		800 —
		Check no. 3			
	15	Notes Payable	220	300 —	
		Cash	110		300 —
		Check no. 4			
	31	Cash	110	2000 —	
		S. Torgue, Capital	310		2000 —
		Deposit no. 2			

2)

Cash

ACCOUNT NO. 110

Date		Item	Ref.	Debit	Credit	Balance Debit	Balance Credit
19--							
Aug	1		J1	10000 —		10000 —	
	2		J1		2000 —	8000 —	
	5		J1		200 —	7800 —	
	15		J1		800 —	7000 —	
	15		J1		300 —	6700 —	
	31		J1	2000 —		8700 —	

Tools

ACCOUNT NO. 120

Date		Item	Ref.	Debit	Credit	Balance Debit	Balance Credit
19--							
Aug	1		J1	800 —		800 —	

Truck

ACCOUNT NO. 130

Date		Item	Ref.	Debit	Credit	Balance Debit	Balance Credit
19--							
Aug	2		J1	10000 —		10000 —	

Accounts Payable

ACCOUNT NO. 210

Date		Item	Ref.	Debit	Credit	Balance Debit	Balance Credit
19--							
Aug	1		J1		800 —		800 —
	15		J1	800 —			-0-

Notes Payable — *ACCOUNT NO.* 220

Date		Item	Ref.	Debit	Credit	Balance Debit	Balance Credit
19--							
Aug	2		J1		8000 —		8000 —
	15		J1		300 —		7700 —

S. Torgue, Capital — *ACCOUNT NO.* 310

Date		Item	Ref.	Debit	Credit	Balance Debit	Balance Credit
19--							
Aug	1		J1		10000 —		10000 —
	31		J1		2000 —		12000 —

S. Torgue, Withdrawal — *ACCOUNT NO.* 320

Date		Item	Ref.	Debit	Credit	Balance Debit	Balance Credit
19--							
Aug	5		J1	200 —		200 —	

3)

Torgue Company
Trial Balance

A/C #	Account	Debit	Credit
	Cash	8700 —	
	Tools	800 —	
	Truck	10000 —	
	Accounts Payable		-0-
	Notes Payable		7700 —
	S. Torgue, Capital		12000 —
	S. Torgue, Withdrawal	200 —	
		19700 —	19700 —

4) 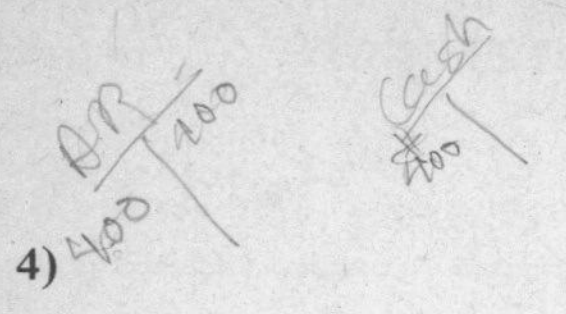

Torgue Company
Balance Sheet
August 31, 19--

Assets		Liabilities	
Cash	$ 8700--	Accounts Payable	-0-
Tools	800--	Notes Payable	7700--
Truck	10000--	Owner's Equity	
		Torgue, Capital	11800--
Total Assets	19500--	Total Liabilities & Owner's Equity	19500--

Name ______________________ **PROBLEM 2.B.6. & ALTERNATE**

Section ____________ Date ____________

1) **General Journal** *PAGE*

Date		Account Names and Explanations	A/C #	Debit	Credit
19--					
July	2	Cash		400 —	
		Accounts Receivable			400 —
		Deposit No. 210			
	10	Cash		300 —	
		Revenue			300 —
		Deposit No. 211			
	15	Rent expense		250 —	
		Cash			250 —
		Check No. 1225			
	15	Accounts Payable (Axon Service)		180 —	
		Cash			180 —
		Check No. 1226			
	19	Cash		520 —	
		Revenue			520 —
		Deposit No. 212			
	25	Michael Dewey, Withdrawal Account		600 —	
		Cash			600 —
		Check No. 1227			
	31	Wage expense		820 —	
		Cash			820 —
		Check No. 1228			
	31	Gasoline expense		150 —	
		Accounts Payable			150 —
		Axon service station			
	31	Accounts Receivable		950 —	
		Revenue			950 —
		To be collected in August			
	31	Truck expense		140 —	
		Accum. Depreciation, Truck			140 —

300
520
950
1770

2)

Dewey Company

Income Statement

July 31, 19--

Revenue		$ 1770 —
Expenses		
Rent Expense	$ 250 —	
Wage Expense	820 —	
Gasoline Expense	150 —	
Depreciation Expence	140 —	1360 —
Net Income		$ 410 —

Name ______________________ PROBLEM 2.B.7. & ALTERNATE

Section ____________ Date ____________

General Journal PAGE

Date		Account Names and Explanations	A/C #	Debit	Credit
19--					
April	3	Accounts Payable		350 —	
		Cash			350 —
		Check no. 560			
	5	Margaret Fong, Withdrawal Acct.		500 —	
		Cash			500 —
		Check no. 561			
	8	Cash		260 —	
		Accounts Receivable			260 —
		Deposit no. 140			
	10	Cash		400 —	
		Revenue			400 —
		Deposit no. 141			
	10	Equipment		4000 —	
		Cash			1000 —
		Notes Payable			3000 —
		Check no. 562			
	18	Rent expense		600 —	
		Cash			600 —
		Check no. 563			
	30	Wage expense		1200 —	
		Cash			1200 —
		Check no. 564			
	30	Utilities expense		90 —	
		Accounts Payable			90 —
	30	Accounts Receivable		2600 —	
		Revenue			2600 —
		To be collected in May			
	30	Depreciation Expense		210 —	
		Accum. Depreciation, Equipment			210 —

Name ____________________ **PROBLEM 2.B.8.** *(ALTERNATE ON REVERSE SIDE)*

Section ____________ Date ____________

1) **General Journal** *PAGE* 1

Date 19..		Account Names and Explanations	A/C #	Debit	Credit
Jan.	2	Cash	11	4000	
		K. Totsy, Capital	31		4000
		Owner invested cash; Deposit No. 1.			
	3	Equipment	16	3000	
		Cash	11		1000
		Notes Payable	26		2000
		Purchased equipment for cash and note; Check No. 101.			
	3	Supplies on Hand	13	600	
		Accounts Payable	21		600
		Purchased supplies on account from George Co.			
	10	Cash	11	700	
		Service Revenue	41		700
		Cash revenue received; Deposit No. 2.			
	15	Rent Expense	51	200	
		Cash	11		200
		Paid January rent; Check No. 102.			
	20	Cash	11	900	
		Service Revenue	41		900
		Cash revenue received; Deposit No. 3.			
	25	K. Totsy, Withdrawals	32	300	
		Cash	11		300
		Owner withdrew cash for personal use; Check No. 103.			
	31	Wage Expense	52	1000	
		Cash	11		1000
		Paid January wages; Check No. 104.			
	31	Accounts Receivable	12	800	
		Service Revenue	41		800
		Billed customers for services performed in January.			
	31	Supplies Expense	53	200	
		Supplies on Hand	13		200
		Supplies used in January.			
	31	Depreciation Expense	54	100	
		Accum. Depr.—Equipment			100
		Depreciation for January.			

1) **General Journal** PAGE 1

Date 19–		Account Names and Explanations	A/C #	Debit	Credit
Mar.	2	Cash		5000	
		G. Scott, Capital			5000
		Owner invested cash; Deposit No. 10.			
	4	Equipment		4000	
		Cash			500
		Notes Payable			3500
		Purchased equipment for cash and note; Check No. 210.			
	5	Supplies on Hand		500	
		Accounts Payable			500
		Purchased supplies on account from B&B.			
	10	Cash		800	
		Service Revenue			800
		Cash revenue received; Deposit No. 11.			
	15	Rent Expense		250	
		Cash			250
		Paid March rent; Check No. 211.			
	21	Cash		750	
		Service Revenue			750
		Cash revenue received; Deposit No. 12.			
	26	G. Scott, Withdrawals		500	
		Cash			500
		Owner withdrew cash for personal use; Check No. 212.			
	31	Wage Expense		1500	
		Cash			1500
		Paid March wages; Check No. 213.			
	31	Accounts Receivable		930	
		Service Revenue			930
		Billed customers for services performed in March.			
	31	Supplies Expense		175	
		Supplies on Hand			175
		Supplied used in March.			
	31	Depreciation Expense		200	
		Accumulated Depreciation–Equipment			200
		Depreciation for March.			

Name ____________________

Section __________ Date __________

Cash

ACCOUNT NO. **11**

Date		Item	Ref.	Debit	Credit	Balance Debit	Balance Credit
19--							
Jan	2		J1	4000—		4000—	
	3		J1		1000—	3000—	
	10		J1	700—		3700—	
	15		J1		200—	3500—	
	20		J1	900—		4400—	
	25		J1		300—	4100—	
	31		J1		1000—	3100—	

Accounts Receivable

ACCOUNT NO. **12**

Date		Item	Ref.	Debit	Credit	Balance Debit	Balance Credit
19--							
Jan	31		J1	800—		800—	

Supplies on Hand

ACCOUNT NO. **13**

Date		Item	Ref.	Debit	Credit	Balance Debit	Balance Credit
19--							
Jan	3		J1	600—		600—	
	31		J1		200—	400—	

Equipment

ACCOUNT NO. **16**

Date		Item	Ref.	Debit	Credit	Balance Debit	Balance Credit
19--							
Jan	3		J1	3000—		3000—	

Accumulated Depreciation—Equipment *ACCOUNT NO.* **016**

Date		Item	Ref.	Debit	Credit	Balance Debit	Balance Credit
19--							
Jan	31		J1		100 —		100 —

Accounts Payable *ACCOUNT NO* **21**

Date		Item	Ref.	Debit	Credit	Balance Debit	Balance Credit
19--							
Jan	3		J1		600 —		600 —

Notes Payable *ACCOUNT NO.* **26**

Date		Item	Ref.	Debit	Credit	Balance Debit	Balance Credit
19--							
Jan	3		J1		2000 —		2000 —

K, Totsy **, Capital** *ACCOUNT NO.* **31**

Date		Item	Ref.	Debit	Credit	Balance Debit	Balance Credit
19--							
Jan	2		J1		4000 —		4000 —

K. Totsy **, Withdrawals** *ACCOUNT NO.* **32**

Date		Item	Ref.	Debit	Credit	Balance Debit	Balance Credit
19--							
Jan	25		J1	300 —		300 —	

Name ____________________ PROBLEM 2.B.8. & ALTERNATE *(Continued)*

Section ____________ Date ____________

Service Revenue *ACCOUNT NO.* 41

Date		Item	Ref.	Debit	Credit	Balance Debit	Balance Credit
19--							
Jan	10		J1		700 —		700 —
	20		J1		900 —		1600 —
	31		J1		800 —		2400 —

Rent Expense *ACCOUNT NO.* 51

Date		Item	Ref.	Debit	Credit	Balance Debit	Balance Credit
19--							
Jan	15		J1	200 —		200 —	

Wage Expense *ACCOUNT NO.* 52

Date		Item	Ref.	Debit	Credit	Balance Debit	Balance Credit
19--							
Jan.	31		J1	1000 —		1000 —	

Supplies Expense *ACCOUNT NO.* 53

Date		Item	Ref.	Debit	Credit	Balance Debit	Balance Credit
19--							
Jan	31		J1	200 —		200 —	

Depreciation Expense *ACCOUNT NO.* 54

Date		Item	Ref.	Debit	Credit	Balance Debit	Balance Credit
19-							
Jan	31		J1	100 —		100 —	

2)

Totsy Company
Trial Balance
Jan 31, 19--

A/C #	Account	Debit	Credit
11	Cash	3100 —	
12	Accounts Receivable	800 —	
13	Supplies on hand	400 —	
16	Equipment	3000 —	
016	Accum. Depreciation - Equipment		100 —
21	Accounts Payable		600 —
26	Notes Payable		2000 —
31	K. Totsy, Capital		4000 —
32	K. Totsy, Withdrawals	300 —	
41	Service Revenue		2400 —
51	Rent Expense	200 —	
52	Wage Expense	1000 —	
53	Supplies Expense	200 —	
54	Depreciation Expense	100 —	
		9100 —	9100 —

3)

Totsy Company
Income Statement
January 19--

Service Revenue		$ 2400 —
Expenses		
Rent Expense	$ 200 —	
Wage Expense	1000 —	
Supplies Expense	200 —	
Depreciation Expense	100 —	1500 —
Net Income		$ 900 —

Name ______________________

Section ____________ Date ____________

4)

Totsy Company
Statement of Owner's Capital
January, 19--

Owner's capital January 1	$ -0-
Investment by Owner	4000 -
Withdrawals	(300 -)
Net Income	900 -
Owner's capital January 31, 19--	$ 4600 -

5)

Totsy Company
Balance Sheet
Jan 31, 19--

Assets			Liabilities		
Cash		$ 3100 —	Accounts Payable		$ 600 —
Accounts Receivable		800 —	Notes Payable		2000 —
Supplies on hand		400 —	Owners Equity		
Equipment	$ 3000		Totsey, Capital		4600 —
Less: Accum Depreciation	100	2900 —			
Total Assets		$ 7200 —	Total Liabilities + Owner's Equity		$ 7200 —

Name ______________________ **PROBLEM 2.B.9.**

Section __________ Date __________

1)

2)

ZAMOST SERVICE COMPANY
Trial Balance
May 31, 19--

	Debit	Credit

Name ______________________

Section ____________ Date ____________

PROBLEM 2.1. & ALTERNATE

1) **General Journal** *PAGE*

Date		Account Names and Explanations	A/C #	Debit	Credit

2)

Name ______________________

Section ____________ Date ____________

3)

Trial Balance

A/C #	Account	Debit	Credit

4)

Income Statement

Name ______________________

Section ____________ Date ____________

PROBLEM 2.2. & ALTERNATE

1) **General Journal** *PAGE*

Date		Account Names and Explanations	A/C #	Debit	Credit

2)

ACCOUNT NO.

Date	Item	Ref.	Debit	Credit	Balance	
					Debit	*Credit*

ACCOUNT NO.

Date	Item	Ref.	Debit	Credit	Balance	
					Debit	*Credit*

ACCOUNT NO.

Date	Item	Ref.	Debit	Credit	Balance	
					Debit	*Credit*

ACCOUNT NO.

Date	Item	Ref.	Debit	Credit	Balance	
					Debit	*Credit*

ACCOUNT NO.

Date	Item	Ref.	Debit	Credit	Balance	
					Debit	*Credit*

Name ______________________

Section ____________ Date ____________

ACCOUNT NO.

Date	Item	Ref.	Debit	Credit	Balance	
					Debit	*Credit*

ACCOUNT NO.

Date	Item	Ref.	Debit	Credit	Balance	
					Debit	*Credit*

ACCOUNT NO.

Date	Item	Ref.	Debit	Credit	Balance	
					Debit	*Credit*

ACCOUNT NO.

Date	Item	Ref.	Debit	Credit	Balance	
					Debit	*Credit*

ACCOUNT NO.

Date	Item	Ref.	Debit	Credit	Balance	
					Debit	*Credit*

3)

Trial Balance

A/C #	Account	Debit	Credit

4)

Income Statement

Name ______________________________

Section ______________ Date __________

Statement of Owner's Capital

Balance Sheet

Name

Section Date

1) **General Journal** *PAGE* 1

Date		Account Names and Explanations	A/C #	Debit	Credit

General Journal *PAGE* 2

Date		Account Names and Explanations	A/C #	Debit	Credit

Name ______________________

Section ____________ Date ____________

2)

ACCOUNT NO.

Date		Item	Ref.	Debit	Credit	Balance	
						Debit	*Credit*

ACCOUNT NO.

Date		Item	Ref.	Debit	Credit	Balance	
						Debit	*Credit*

ACCOUNT NO.

Date		Item	Ref.	Debit	Credit	Balance	
						Debit	*Credit*

ACCOUNT NO.

Date		Item	Ref.	Debit	Credit	Balance	
						Debit	*Credit*

ACCOUNT NO.

Date	Item	Ref.	Debit	Credit	Balance	
					Debit	*Credit*

ACCOUNT NO.

Date	Item	Ref.	Debit	Credit	Balance	
					Debit	*Credit*

ACCOUNT NO.

Date	Item	Ref.	Debit	Credit	Balance	
					Debit	*Credit*

ACCOUNT NO.

Date	Item	Ref.	Debit	Credit	Balance	
					Debit	*Credit*

Name ______________________________

Section ______________ Date ____________

ACCOUNT NO.

Date		Item	Ref.	Debit	Credit	Balance	
						Debit	*Credit*

ACCOUNT NO.

Date		Item	Ref.	Debit	Credit	Balance	
						Debit	*Credit*

ACCOUNT NO.

Date		Item	Ref.	Debit	Credit	Balance	
						Debit	*Credit*

ACCOUNT NO.

Date		Item	Ref.	Debit	Credit	Balance	
						Debit	*Credit*

ACCOUNT NO.

Date		Item	Ref.	Debit	Credit	Balance	
						Debit	*Credit*

ACCOUNT NO.

Date		Item	Ref.	Debit	Credit	Balance	
						Debit	*Credit*

ACCOUNT NO.

Date		Item	Ref.	Debit	Credit	Balance	
						Debit	*Credit*

ACCOUNT NO.

Date		Item	Ref.	Debit	Credit	Balance	
						Debit	*Credit*

ACCOUNT NO.

Date		Item	Ref.	Debit	Credit	Balance	
						Debit	*Credit*

Name ______________________ **PROBLEM 2.3. & ALTERNATE** ***(Continued)***

Section __________ Date __________

3)

Trial Balance

A/C #	**Account**	**Debit**	**Credit**

4)

Income Statement

Statement of Owner's Capital

Balance Sheet

Name ____________________ **COMPREHENSION PROBLEM 2.4.**

Section ____________ Date ____________

1)

Cash

Mortgage Payable

Equipment

K. Muster, Capital

Building

K. Muster, Withdrawals

Land

2) **General Journal** *PAGE*

Date		Account Names and Explanations	A/C #	Debit	Credit

Name ______________________

Section ____________ Date __________

1)

MILO BARGARINO, ATTORNEY
Balance Sheet
May 31, 19--

MILO BARGARINO, ATTORNEY
Balance Sheet
June 30, 19--

2)

MILO BARGARINO, ATTORNEY
Schedule of Cash Flow
For the Month of June, 19--

Name ______________________

Section ____________ Date ____________

COMPREHENSION PROBLEM 2.6.

General Journal

PAGE 11

Date		Account Names and Explanations	A/C #	Debit	Credit

General Journal

PAGE 12

Date		Account Names and Explanations	A/C #	Debit	Credit

Name ______________________________

Section ______________ Date ____________

General Journal

PAGE 13

Date		Account Names and Explanations	A/C #	Debit	Credit

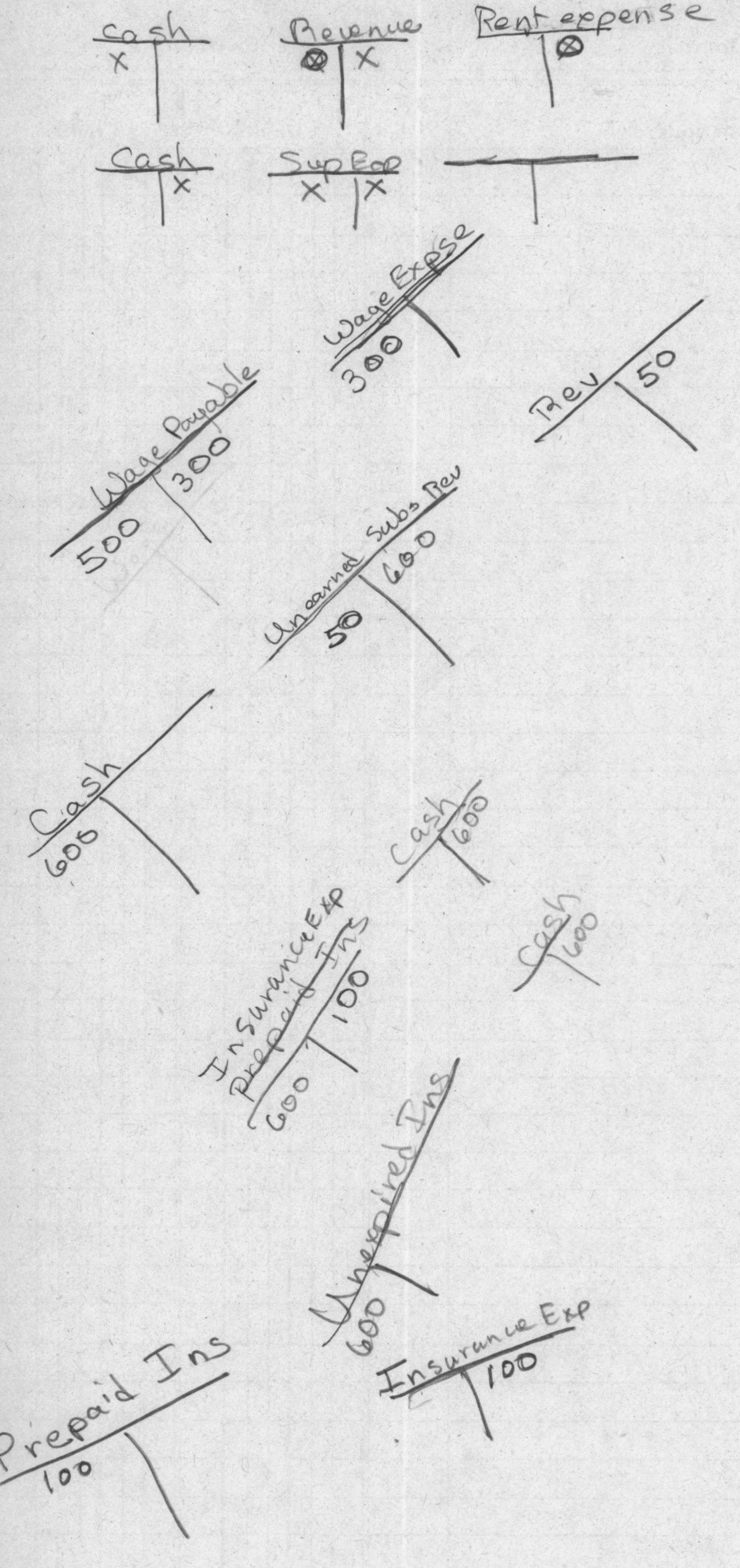

Cash
X
Revenue
X
Rent expense
Cash
X
Sup Exp
X
X
Wage Expse
300
Rev
50
Wage Payable
500
300
Unearned Subs Rev
50
600
Cash
600
Cash
600
Cash
600
Insurance Exp
Prepaid Ins
600
100
Unexpired Ins
600
Insurance Exp
100
Prepaid Ins
100

Name ______________________ **SELF-QUIZ FOR SECTION 3.A**

Section ____________ Date __________

1.	Asset	Liability	Expense	Revenue
a		increase	~~increase~~	decrease
b	increase		decrease	~~increase~~
c	decrease		increase	
d	decrease		increase	
e	increase	~~decrease~~		~~decrease~~ increase
f		decrease		increase
g		~~decrease~~ increase	increase	
h		~~decrease~~ increase	increase	

2. **General Journal** *PAGE* J1

Date		Account Names and Explanations	A/C #	Debit	Credit
19--					
May	31	Wage expense		300 —	
		Wages Payable			300 —
~~June~~	~~3~~	~~Wages Payable~~		~~500~~ —	
		~~Cash~~			~~500~~
		~~Employee wages for week~~			
3 June	1	Cash		600 —	
		Unearned Subscription Revenue			600 —
		Twelve month subscription			
	30	Unearned Subscription Revenue		50 —	
		Revenue			50 —
4. July	1	Prepaid Insurance		100 —	
a.		Insurance Expense			100 —
	31	Insurance Expense		100 —	
b.		Prepaid Insurance			100 —

General Journal PAGE

Date		Account Names and Explanations	A/C #	Debit	Credit
19— Sept	30	Depreciation Expense—Truck		300—	
		Accum. Depreciation—Truck			300—

Name ______________________ **PROBLEM 3.A.6. & ALTERNATE**

Section ____________ Date ____________

General Journal *PAGE* 1

Date		Account Names and Explanations	A/C #	Debit	Credit
19--					
June	30	Accounts Receivable		85 —	
		Service Revenue			85 —
		earned last day of June to be billed 7/3			
	30	Wage expense		500 —	
		Wages Payable			500 —
		earned in June payable 7/2			
	30	Supplies expense		215 —	
		Office supplies			215 —
		Supplies used in June			
	30	Depreciation expense - automobile		150 —	
		Accum. Depreciation - automobile			150 —
		One months depreciation			

Name ____________________

Section ____________ Date ____________

PROBLEM 3.A.7. & ALTERNATE

General Journal

PAGE

Date		Account Names and Explanations	A/C #	Debit	Credit

Name ______________________ **PROBLEM 3.A.8.**

Section ____________ Date ____________

General Journal *PAGE*

Date		Account Names and Explanations	A/C #	Debit	Credit
		1) Able Company			
		2) Baker Company			

Name ____________________ PROBLEM 3.A.9.

Section __________ Date __________

General Journal PAGE 1

Date		Account Names and Explanations	A/C #	Debit	Credit
19--		**1) Conner Company**			
Oct.	1	Rent expense		3000 —	
		Cash			3000 —
		Rent for Oct, Nov, Dec			
	31	Prepaid rent		2000 —	
		Rent expense			2000 —
Oct	1	Prepaid Insurance ~~Accounts Payable~~		3000 —	
		Cash			3000 —
	31	Rent ~~Expenses~~		1000 —	
		Prepaid Insurance			1000 —
19--		**Duncan Company**			
Oct.	1	Cash		3000 —	
		Rent Revenue			3000 —
		Rent from Conner Co - Oct, Nov, Dec			
	31	Rent Revenue		2000 —	
		Unearned rent revenue ~~payable~~			2000 —
Oct	1	Cash		3000 —	
		Unearned Insurance ~~Accounts Payable~~			3000
	31	Unearned Insurance		1000 —	
					1000 —

General Journal *PAGE*

Date		Account Names and Explanations	A/C #	Debit	Credit
		2) Conner Company			
		Duncan Company			

Name ______________________ **PROBLEM 3.A.10.**

Section __________ Date __________

1) **General Journal** *PAGE*

Date		Account Names and Explanations	A/C #	Debit	Credit

2)

RABANKS RESEARCH COMPANY
Adjusted Trial Balance
December 31, 19--

	Debit	Credit

Name ____________________

Section __________ Date __________

3)

RABANKS RESEARCH COMPANY
Income Statement
For the Year Ended December 31, 19--

RABANKS RESEARCH COMPANY
Balance Sheet
December 31, 19--

Name ______________________

Section ____________ Date ____________

1. A ten-column work sheet for this requirement can be found at the back of this volume.

2.

DIBBS COMPANY
Income Statement
For the Month of April, 19--

Service Revenue		
Wage Expense		
Supplies Expense		
Depreciation Expense		
Net Income		

DIBBS COMPANY
Statement of Owner's Capital
For the Month of April, 19--

B. Dibbs, Capital April 1, 19--		
Withdrawals		
Net Income		
B. Dibbs, Capital April 31, 19--		

DIBBS COMPANY
Balance Sheet
April 30, 19--

Name ______________________

Section ______________ Date __________

3.

Name

Section Date

PROBLEM 3.B.4. & ALTERNATE

1) A ten-column work sheet for this requirement can be found at the back of this volume.

2) Link Company

Income Statement

March 31 19--

Fees Earned		$ 2150—
Rent Expense	$ 700—	
Interest Expense	40—	
Supplies Expense	70—	
Depreciation Expense	170—	980—
Net Income		$ 1170—

Link Company, Capital

Statement of Owner's Capital

March 31, 19--

Link Company, Capital March 31, 19--	$ 2550—
Investments by Owner	-0-
Withdrawals	(500—)
Net Income	1170—
Link Company, Capital March 31, 19--	$ 3220—

Link Company
Balance Sheet
March 31, 19--

Assets		
Current		
Cash	$ 600 —	
Accounts Receivable	1150 —	
Supplies	20 —	
Truck	6800 —	
Accumulated Depreciation		510 —
Liabilities		
Accounts Payable		800 —
Interest Payable		40 —
Note Payable		4000 —
Owners Equity		
F. Link, Capital		3220 —
Total Assets; Liabilities + O.E.	8570 —	8570 —

Name ____________________

Section ____________ Date ____________

3) **General Journal** *PAGE*

Date		Account Names and Explanations	A/C #	Debit	Credit

Name ______________________________

Section ______________ Date ____________

PROBLEM 3.B.5.

1) and 3) A partially completed ten-column work sheet for these requirements can be found at the back of this volume.

2)

Name

Section Date

PROBLEM 3.B.6.

1)

2) A ten-column work sheet for this requirement can be found at the back of this volume.

Name ______________________

Section ____________ Date __________

PROBLEM 3.B.7.

STARBADS REPAIR

Work Sheet

For the Month of June, 19--

A/C #	Account	Adjusted Trial Balance		Income Statement		Balance Sheet	
		Dr.	*Cr.*	*Dr.*	*Cr.*	*Dr.*	*Cr.*

Name ______________________________

Section ______________ Date ____________

1.

General Journal

PAGE 28

Date		Account Names and Explanations	A/C #	Debit	Credit

H. Van Allen, Capital *ACCOUNT NO.* 31

Date		Item	Ref.	Debit	Credit	Balance	
						Debit	*Credit*
19–							
Oct.	1	Balance	X				230

H. Van Allen, Withdrawals *ACCOUNT NO.* 32

Date		Item	Ref.	Debit	Credit	Balance	
						Debit	*Credit*
19–							
Oct.	15		27	50		50	
	31		27	550		600	

Service Revenue *ACCOUNT NO.* 41

Date		Item	Ref.	Debit	Credit	Balance	
						Debit	*Credit*
19–							
Oct.	10		27		500		500
	25		27		390		890
	31	Adjusting	27		210		1100

Name ____________________

Section __________ Date __________

Rent Expense *ACCOUNT NO.* **51**

Date		Item	Ref.	Debit	Credit	Balance	
						Debit	*Credit*
19--							
Oct.	15		27	300		300	

Supplies Expense *ACCOUNT NO.* **52**

Date		Item	Ref.	Debit	Credit	Balance	
						Debit	*Credit*
19--							
Oct.	8		27	80		80	
	17		27	70		150	

Name ____________________

Section ____________ Date ____________

PROBLEM 3.C.5. & ALTERNATE

1) **General Journal** *PAGE*

Date		Account Names and Explanations	A/C #	Debit	Credit

2) General Journal *PAGE*

Date		Account Names and Explanations	A/C #	Debit	Credit

Name ______________________________

Section ______________ Date ____________

PROBLEM 3.C.6. & ALTERNATE

1) General Journal

PAGE

Date		Account Names and Explanations	A/C #	Debit	Credit

2)

Post-Closing Trial Balance

A/C #	Account	Debit	Credit

Name ______________________________ **PROBLEM 3.C.7.**

Section ______________ Date ______________

1) **General Journal** *PAGE*

Date		Account Names and Explanations	A/C #	Debit	Credit

2)

VALLEY CABLE-VISION
Income Statement
For the Month of September, 19--

Name ______________________ **PROBLEM 3.C.8.**

Section ____________ Date ____________

1) **General Journal** *PAGE*

Date		Account Names and Explanations	A/C #	Debit	Credit

2)

CITY REPAIR SERVICE
Balance Sheet
July 31, 19--

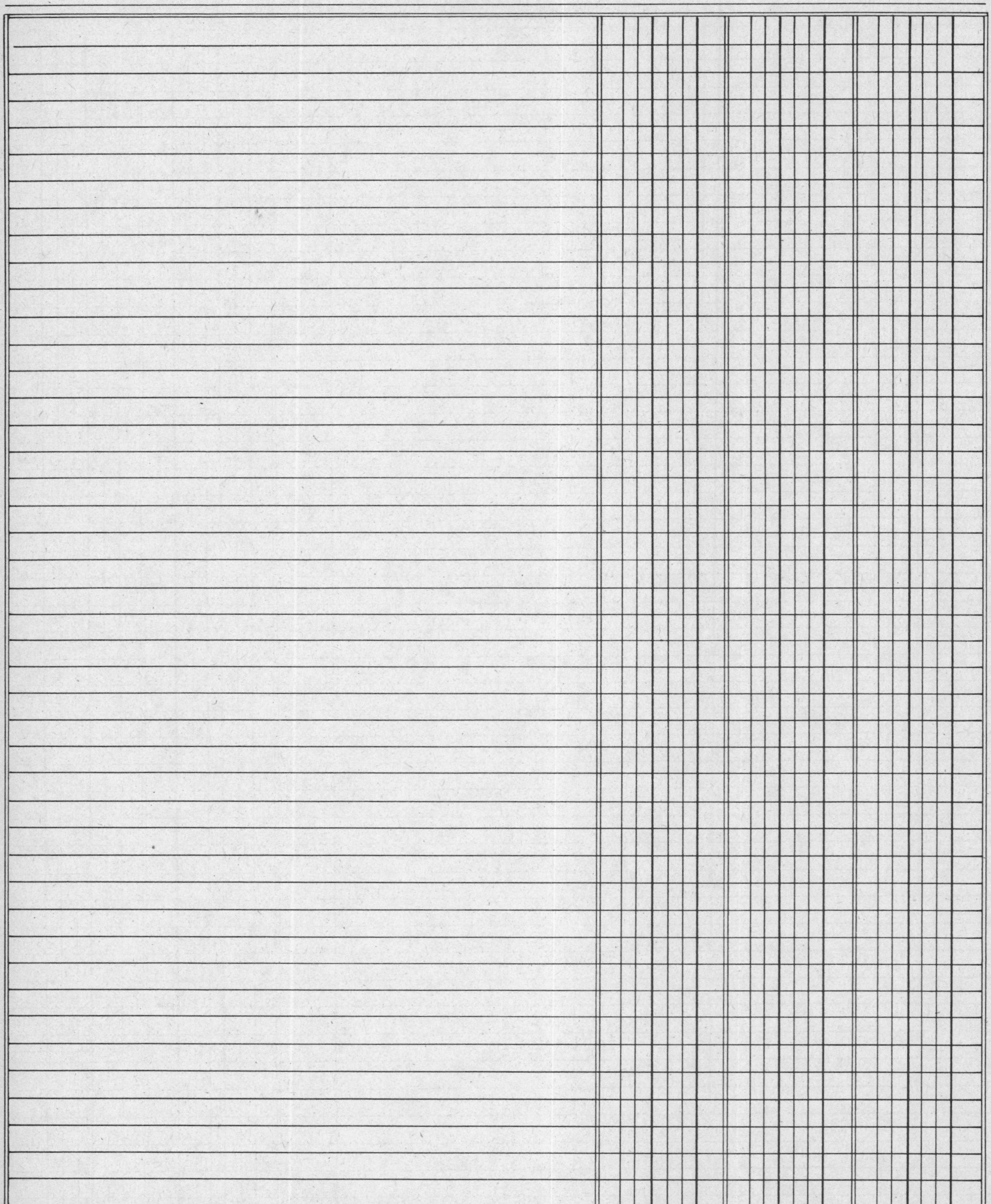

Name ____________________ **PROBLEM 3.C.9.**

Section ____________ Date ____________

1) **General Journal** *PAGE* 84

Date		Account Names and Explanations	A/C #	Debit	Credit

2)

M. Madre, Capital — *ACCOUNT NO.* **311**

Date		Item	Ref.	Debit	Credit	Balance Debit	Balance Credit
19--							
Dec.	1	Balance	X				2000

M. Madre, Withdrawals — *ACCOUNT NO.* **312**

Date		Item	Ref.	Debit	Credit	Balance Debit	Balance Credit
19--							
Dec.	14		82	400		400	
	30		83	400		800	

Fees Earned — *ACCOUNT NO.* **411**

Date		Item	Ref.	Debit	Credit	Balance Debit	Balance Credit
19--							
Dec.	30	Balance from preceding ledger page	X				8000

Name ________________________________ **PROBLEM 3.C.9.** ***(Continued)***

Section ______________ Date ______________

Rent Expense *ACCOUNT NO.* **511**

Date		Item	Ref.	Debit	Credit	Balance Debit	Balance Credit
19--							
Dec.	1		81	1 200		1 200	

Wage Expense *ACCOUNT NO.* **512**

Date		Item	Ref.	Debit	Credit	Balance Debit	Balance Credit
19--							
Dec.	15		82	2 500		2 500	
	31		83	2 500		5 000	

Supplies Expense *ACCOUNT NO.* **513**

Date		Item	Ref.	Debit	Credit	Balance Debit	Balance Credit
19--							
Dec.	5		81	120		120	
	20		82	60		180	

Depreciation Expense *ACCOUNT NO.* **514**

Date		Item	Ref.	Debit	Credit	Balance Debit	Balance Credit
19--							
Dec.	31	Adjusting	83	140		140	

For use by students that choose to close amounts through an Income Summary account.

Income Summary *ACCOUNT NO.* **400**

Date		Item	Ref.	Debit	Credit	Balance Debit	Balance Credit

3)

MADRE COMPANY
Post-Closing Trial Balance
December 31, 19--

A/C #	Account	Debit	Credit

Name ______________________________

Section ______________ Date ____________

PROBLEM 3.1. & ALTERNATE

2) and 3)

General Journal

PAGE

Date		Account Names and Explanations	A/C #	Debit	Credit

6), 7) and 8) **General Journal** *PAGE*

Date		Account Names and Explanations	A/C #	Debit	Credit

Name ____________

Section ________ Date ________

1), 3) and 8)

ACCOUNT NO.

Date		Item	Ref.	Debit	Credit	Balance	
						Debit	*Credit*

ACCOUNT NO.

Date		Item	Ref.	Debit	Credit	Balance	
						Debit	*Credit*

ACCOUNT NO.

Date		Item	Ref.	Debit	Credit	Balance	
						Debit	*Credit*

ACCOUNT NO.

Date	Item	Ref.	Debit	Credit	Balance	
					Debit	*Credit*

ACCOUNT NO.

Date	Item	Ref.	Debit	Credit	Balance	
					Debit	*Credit*

ACCOUNT NO.

Date	Item	Ref.	Debit	Credit	Balance	
					Debit	*Credit*

ACCOUNT NO.

Date	Item	Ref.	Debit	Credit	Balance	
					Debit	*Credit*

ACCOUNT NO.

Date	Item	Ref.	Debit	Credit	Balance	
					Debit	*Credit*

Name ______________________

Section ____________ Date ____________

ACCOUNT NO.

Date	Item	Ref.	Debit	Credit	Balance	
					Debit	*Credit*

ACCOUNT NO.

Date	Item	Ref.	Debit	Credit	Balance	
					Debit	*Credit*

ACCOUNT NO.

Date	Item	Ref.	Debit	Credit	Balance	
					Debit	*Credit*

ACCOUNT NO.

Date	Item	Ref.	Debit	Credit	Balance	
					Debit	*Credit*

ACCOUNT NO.

Date		Item	Ref.	Debit	Credit	Balance	
						Debit	*Credit*

ACCOUNT NO.

Date		Item	Ref.	Debit	Credit	Balance	
						Debit	*Credit*

ACCOUNT NO.

Date		Item	Ref.	Debit	Credit	Balance	
						Debit	*Credit*

ACCOUNT NO.

Date		Item	Ref.	Debit	Credit	Balance	
						Debit	*Credit*

ACCOUNT NO.

Date		Item	Ref.	Debit	Credit	Balance	
						Debit	*Credit*

Name ____________________

Section ______________ Date ______________

ACCOUNT NO.

Date		Item	Ref.	Debit	Credit	Balance	
						Debit	*Credit*

ACCOUNT NO.

Date		Item	Ref.	Debit	Credit	Balance	
						Debit	*Credit*

ACCOUNT NO.

Date		Item	Ref.	Debit	Credit	Balance	
						Debit	*Credit*

For use by students that choose to close accounts through an Income Summary account.

Income Summary

ACCOUNT NO.

Date		Item	Ref.	Debit	Credit	Balance	
						Debit	*Credit*

4) A ten-column work sheet for this requirement can be found at the back of this volume.

5)

Income Statement

Statement of Owner's Capital

Name ____________________

Section ______________ Date ____________

Balance Sheet

Name ______________________________ **PROBLEM 3.2. & ALTERNATE**

Section ______________ Date ____________

1) A partially completed ten-column work sheet for this requirement can be found at the back of this volume.

2)

Income Statement

Statement of Owner's Capital

3)

Balance Sheet

Name ______________________

Section ____________ Date ____________

4) **General Journal** *PAGE*

Date		Account Names and Explanations	A/C #	Debit	Credit

General Journal

PAGE

Date		Account Names and Explanations	A/C #	Debit	Credit

5)

Post-Closing Trial Balance

A/C #	Account	Debit	Credit

Name ____________________

Section ____________ Date ____________

PROBLEM 3.3. & ALTERNATE

1) A ten-column work sheet for this requirement can be found at the back of this volume.

2), 3) and 4) **General Journal** *PAGE*

Date		Account Names and Explanations	A/C #	Debit	Credit

General Journal *PAGE*

Date		Account Names and Explanations	A/C #	Debit	Credit

Name ______________________ PROBLEM 3.3. *(Continued)*

Section __________ Date __________

(Accounts for Alternate 3.3. begin on page 153.)

4) **Cash** *ACCOUNT NO.* **111**

Date		Item	Ref.	Debit	Credit	Balance Debit	Balance Credit
19--							
Dec.	1	Balance	X			2000	
	2		42		1300	700	
	3		42	3000		3700	
	7		42	4000		7700	
	15		42		5000	2700	
	16		42		400	2300	
	16		42		1000	1300	
	19		42		100	1200	
	21		42	200		1400	
	30		42		300	1100	

Accounts Receivable *ACCOUNT NO.* **112**

Date		Item	Ref.	Debit	Credit	Balance Debit	Balance Credit
19--							
Dec.	1	Balance	X			3500	
	3		42		3000	500	
	21		42		200	300	
	30		42	3000		3300	

Supplies *ACCOUNT NO.* **113**

Date		Item	Ref.	Debit	Credit	Balance Debit	Balance Credit
19 --							
Dec.	1	Balance	X			400	
	19		42	100		500	
	21		42	800		1300	

Prepaid Insurance — *ACCOUNT NO.* **114**

Date		Item	Ref.	Debit	Credit	Balance	
						Debit	*Credit*
19--							
Dec.	1	Balance	X			50	

Land — *ACCOUNT NO.* **117**

Date		Item	Ref.	Debit	Credit	Balance	
						Debit	*Credit*
19--							
Dec.	1	Balance	X			10000	

Building — *ACCOUNT NO.* **118**

Date		Item	Ref.	Debit	Credit	Balance	
						Debit	*Credit*
19--							
Dec.	1	Balance	X			50000	

Accumulated Depreciation—Building — *ACCOUNT NO.* **0118**

Date		Item	Ref.	Debit	Credit	Balance	
						Debit	*Credit*
19--							
Dec.	1	Balance	X				1100

Name ______________________

Section ____________ Date ____________

PROBLEM 3.3. *(Continued)*

Accounts Payable ACCOUNT NO. 211

Date		Item	Ref.	Debit	Credit	Balance Debit	Balance Credit
19--							
Dec.	1	Balance	X				400
	16		42	400			-0-
	21		42		800		800
	30		42	300			500

Wages Payable ACCOUNT NO. 212

Date		Item	Ref.	Debit	Credit	Balance Debit	Balance Credit
19--							
Dec.	1	Balance	X				300
	2		42	300			-0-

Interest Payable ACCOUNT NO. 213

Date		Item	Ref.	Debit	Credit	Balance Debit	Balance Credit

Mortgage Payable ACCOUNT NO. 218

Date		Item	Ref.	Debit	Credit	Balance Debit	Balance Credit
19--							
Dec.	1	Balance	X				30000

Jo Moore, Capital — *ACCOUNT NO.* **311**

Date		Item	Ref.	Debit	Credit	Balance Debit	Balance Credit
19--							
Dec.	1	Balance	X				34150

Jo Moore, Withdrawals — *ACCOUNT NO.* **312**

Date		Item	Ref.	Debit	Credit	Balance Debit	Balance Credit
19--							
Dec.	15		42	5000		5000	

Service Revenue — *ACCOUNT NO.* **411**

Date		Item	Ref.	Debit	Credit	Balance Debit	Balance Credit
19--							
Dec.	7		42		4000		4000
	30		42		3000		7000

Wage Expense — *ACCOUNT NO.* **511**

Date		Item	Ref.	Debit	Credit	Balance Debit	Balance Credit
19--							
Dec.	2		42	1000		1000	
	16		42	1000		2000	

Name ____________________

Section __________ Date __________

Supplies Expense *ACCOUNT NO.* **512**

Date	Item	Ref.	Debit	Credit	Balance	
					Debit	*Credit*

Insurance Expense *ACCOUNT NO.* **513**

Date	Item	Ref.	Debit	Credit	Balance	
					Debit	*Credit*

Depreciation Expense *ACCOUNT NO.* **514**

Date	Item	Ref.	Debit	Credit	Balance	
					Debit	*Credit*

Interest Expense *ACCOUNT NO.* **515**

Date	Item	Ref.	Debit	Credit	Balance	
					Debit	*Credit*

For use by students that choose to close amounts through an Income Summary account.

Income Summary *ACCOUNT NO.* **313**

Date		Item	Ref.	Debit	Credit	Balance	
						Debit	*Credit*

Name ________________________ **ALTERNATE PROBLEM 3.3.** ***(Continued)***

Section ____________ Date ____________

4)

Cash *ACCOUNT NO.* **111**

Date		Item	Ref.	Debit	Credit	Balance Debit	Balance Credit
19--							
May	1	Balance	X			1500	
	2		20		1300	200	
	3		20	3000		3200	
	15		20	4000		7200	
	15		20		5000	2200	
	16		20		400	1800	
	16		20		1000	800	
	19		20		100	700	
	21		20	200		900	
	30		20		300	600	

Accounts Receivable *ACCOUNT NO.* **112**

Date		Item	Ref.	Debit	Credit	Balance Debit	Balance Credit
19--							
May	1	Balance	X			4000	
	3		20		3000	1000	
	21		20		200	800	

Supplies *ACCOUNT NO.* **113**

Date		Item	Ref.	Debit	Credit	Balance Debit	Balance Credit
19--							
May	1	Balance	X			400	
	19		20	100		500	
	21		20	800		1300	

Prepaid Insurance — *ACCOUNT NO.* **114**

Date		Item	Ref.	Debit	Credit	Balance	
						Debit	*Credit*
19--							
May	1	Balance	X			400	

Land — *ACCOUNT NO.* **116**

Date		Item	Ref.	Debit	Credit	Balance	
						Debit	*Credit*
19--							
May	1	Balance	X			8000	

Building — *ACCOUNT NO.* **117**

Date		Item	Ref.	Debit	Credit	Balance	
						Debit	*Credit*
19--							
May	1	Balance	X			52000	

Accumulated Depreciation—Building — *ACCOUNT NO.* **0117**

Date		Item	Ref.	Debit	Credit	Balance	
						Debit	*Credit*
19--							
May	1	Balance	X				1450

Name ______________________

Section ____________ Date ____________

Accounts Payable *ACCOUNT NO.* **211**

Date		Item	Ref.	Debit	Credit	Balance Debit	Balance Credit
19--							
May	1	Balance	X				400
	16		20	400			-0-
	21		20		800		800
	30		20	300			500

Salaries Payable *ACCOUNT NO.* **212**

Date		Item	Ref.	Debit	Credit	Balance Debit	Balance Credit
19--							
May	1	Balance	X				300
	30		20	300			-0-

Interest Payable *ACCOUNT NO.* **213**

Date		Item	Ref.	Debit	Credit	Balance Debit	Balance Credit

Mortgage Payable *ACCOUNT NO.* **218**

Date		Item	Ref.	Debit	Credit	Balance Debit	Balance Credit
19--							
May	1	Balance	X				32150

M. Barclay, Capital — *ACCOUNT NO.* **311**

Date		Item	Ref.	Debit	Credit	Balance Debit	Balance Credit
19--							
May	1	Balance	X				32000

M. Barclay, Withdrawals — *ACCOUNT NO.* **312**

Date		Item	Ref.	Debit	Credit	Balance Debit	Balance Credit
19--							
May	15		20	5000		5000	

Fees Earned — *ACCOUNT NO.* **411**

Date		Item	Ref.	Debit	Credit	Balance Debit	Balance Credit
19--							
May	15		20		4000		4000

Salaries Expense — *ACCOUNT NO.* **511**

Date		Item	Ref.	Debit	Credit	Balance Debit	Balance Credit
19--							
May	2		20	1000		1000	
	16		20	1000		2000	

Name ______________________

Section __________ Date __________

Supplies Expense ACCOUNT NO. **512**

Date		Item	Ref.	Debit	Credit	Balance Debit	Balance Credit

Insurance Expense ACCOUNT NO. **513**

Date		Item	Ref.	Debit	Credit	Balance Debit	Balance Credit

Depreciation Expense ACCOUNT NO. **514**

Date		Item	Ref.	Debit	Credit	Balance Debit	Balance Credit

Interest Expense ACCOUNT NO. **515**

Date		Item	Ref.	Debit	Credit	Balance Debit	Balance Credit

For use by students that choose to close amounts through an Income Summary account.

Income Summary *ACCOUNT NO.* **313**

Date		Item	Ref.	Debit	Credit	Balance	
						Debit	*Credit*

Name ____________________

Section ____________ Date ____________

COMPREHENSION PROBLEM 3.4.

1)

BUCKETSHOP COMPANY
Balance Sheet
June 30, 19--

2)

Name ______________________________

Section ______________ Date ______________

1) and 2) A ten-column work sheet for these requirements can be found at the back of this volume.

3)

SHUSTER COMPANY
Income Statement
For the Year Ended December 31, 19--

SHUSTER COMPANY
Balance Sheet
December 31, 19--

Name ______________________

Section ____________ Date ________

4)

Name ______________________ **PROBLEM 3.I.1.**

Section ____________ Date ____________

General Journal *PAGE* 11

Date		Account Names and Explanations	A/C #	Debit	Credit

Accounts Receivable *ACCOUNT NO.* **112**

Date		Item	Ref.	Debit	Credit	Balance Debit	Balance Credit
19--							
May	31	Balance	X			1100	
	31	Adjusting	10	1200		2300	

Supplies *ACCOUNT NO.* **113**

Date		Item	Ref.	Debit	Credit	Balance Debit	Balance Credit
19--							
May	31	Balance	X			100	
	31	Adjusting	10		80	20	

Accumulated Depreciation—Truck *ACCOUNT NO.* **0114**

Date		Item	Ref.	Debit	Credit	Balance Debit	Balance Credit
19--							
May	31	Balance	X				3000
	31	Adjusting	10		250		3250

Wages Payable *ACCOUNT NO.* **212**

Date		Item	Ref.	Debit	Credit	Balance Debit	Balance Credit
19--							
May	31	Adjusting	10		300		300

Name ______________________

Section ____________ Date ____________

PROBLEM 3.I.1. *(Continued)*

Interest Payable — *ACCOUNT NO.* **213**

Date		Item	Ref.	Debit	Credit	Balance Debit	Balance Credit
19--							
May	31	Adjusting	10		20		20

Fees Earned — *ACCOUNT NO.* **411**

Date		Item	Ref.	Debit	Credit	Balance Debit	Balance Credit
19--							
May	31	Balance	X				4000
	31	Adjusting	10		1200		5200
	31	Closing	10	5200			-0-

Wage Expense — *ACCOUNT NO.* **511**

Date		Item	Ref.	Debit	Credit	Balance Debit	Balance Credit
19--							
May	31	Balance	X			2000	
	31	Adjusting	10	300		2300	
	31	Closing	10		2300	-0-	

Supplies Expense — *ACCOUNT NO.* **512**

Date		Item	Ref.	Debit	Credit	Balance Debit	Balance Credit
19--							
May	31	Adjusting	10	80		80	
	31	Closing	10		80	-0-	

Interest Expense *ACCOUNT NO.* **513**

Date		Item	Ref.	Debit	Credit	Balance Debit	Balance Credit
19–							
May	31	Adjusting	10	20		20	
	31	Closing	10		20	-0-	

Depreciation Expense *ACCOUNT NO.* **514**

Date		Item	Ref.	Debit	Credit	Balance Debit	Balance Credit
19--							
May	31	Adjusting	10	250		250	
	31	Closing	10		250	-0-	

Name ____________________ **PROBLEM 3.II.7.**

Section ____________ Date ____________

General Journal *PAGE*

Date		Account Names and Explanations	A/C #	Debit	Credit
		1)			
		2)			
		3)			

Name ______________________

PROBLEM 3.II.8.

Section ____________ Date ____________

General Journal *PAGE*

Date		Account Names and Explanations	A/C #	Debit	Credit
		1)			
		2)			
		3)			

General Journal PAGE

Date		Account Names and Explanations	A/C #	Debit	Credit
		4)			
		5)			

Name ______________________

Section __________ Date __________

1. Merchandising is buying goods then reselling them without changing them in any way

2. Retailing is selling merchandise in small quantities to consumers.
Wholesaling is buying goods from manufacturers and selling them to retailers or other merchants.

3. General Journal PAGE

Date		Account Names and Explanations	A/C #	Debit	Credit
Mar	1	Purchases		8000 —	
		Accounts Payable Doby Supply			8000 —
		shipped f.o.b Shipping point			
	2	Purchases		400 —	
		Cash			400 —
		Check no. 262			
	4	Freight In		60 —	
		Cash			60 —
		CK no. 5063 Doby Supply Co. 3/1			
	5	Cash		500 —	
		Sales			500 —
		Deposit no. 1055			
	7	Accounts Receivable - Jay Mooney		4000 —	
		Sales			4000 —
		f.o.b. destination			

General Journal *PAGE*

Date		Account Names and Explanations	A/C #	Debit	Credit
Mar	8	Freight Out		40 —	
		Cash			40 —
		CK no. 5064			
	9	Accounts Payable - Doby Supply Co.		8000 —	
		Cash			8000 —
		CK no. 5065			
	14	Cash		4000 —	
		Accounts Receivable Jay Mooney			4000 —
		Deposit no. 1056			

4.

INLAND SALES COMPANY
Schedule of Cost of Goods Sold
For the Year Ended December 31, 19X5

Merchandise Inventory 12/31/X4		40000 —
Purchases	500000 —	
Transportation In	10000 —	
Delivered cost of purchases		510000 —
Cost of goods available for sale		550000 —
Merchandise Inventory 12/31/X5		30000 —
Cost of goods sold		520000 —

Name ______________________ PROBLEM 4.A.6. & ALTERNATE

Section __________ Date __________

General Journal PAGE

Date		Account Names and Explanations	A/C #	Debit	Credit
19--					
May	1	Purchases		1000 —	
		Cash			1000 —
		Check no. 1188			
		f.o.b. destination			
	8	Purchases		2000 —	
		Accounts Payable			2000 —
		f.o.b. shipping point			
	13	Transportation in (or freight in)		40 —	
		Cash			40 —
		Paid freight on May 8 purchases			
		Check no. 1189			
	14	Cash		800 —	
		Sales			800 —
		Deposit no. 650			
	20	Accounts Receivable		5000 —	
		Sales			5000 —
		f.o.b. destination			
	23	Transportation out (or freight out)		50 —	
		Cash			50 —
		Paid freight on May 20 sales			
		Check no. 1190			

Name ______________________ **PROBLEM 4.A.7. & ALTERNATE**

Section ____________ Date ____________

Woltzing Company

Schedule of Cost of Goods Sold

For Month ending June 30 19--

Merchandise Inventory, June 1		$21 000 —
Purchases	$220 000 —	
Freight in	3 800 —	
Delivered cost of purchases		223 800 —
Cost of goods available for sale		244 800 —
Merchandise Inventory, June 30		30 000 —
Cost of goods sold		$214 800 —

Name ______________________________

Section ________________ Date ____________

PROBLEM 4.A.8. & ALTERNATE

General Journal *PAGE*

Date		Account Names and Explanations	A/C #	Debit	Credit
19--		1) Purchases		300 —	
Sept	3	Accounts Payable			300 —
		Purchased from Giant Wholesalers			
		f.o.b. shipping point			
	8	Transportation in (or freight in)		15 00	
		Cash			15 00
		Freight on Sept. 3 purchases			
	12	Purchases		5000 —	
		Accounts Payable			5000 —
		Purchased from Giant Wholesalers			
		f.o.b. destination			
		2)			
Sept	3	Accounts Receivable		300 —	
		Sales			300 —
		A R		15 —	
		Sales			15 —
		Freight Out		50 —	
		Cash			50 —

Name ______________________

Section ____________ Date __________

PROBLEM 4.A.9.

1)

2)

Name ______________________

Section ____________ Date ____________

1.

General Journal

PAGE

Date		Account Names and Explanations	A/C #	Debit	Credit
19--					
Apr.	4	Purchases		3000 —	
		Accounts Payable			3000 —
		From Duke Company 2/10, n/30			
	6	Accounts Receivable		600 —	
		Sales			600 —
		Ray Company, 1/10, n/60			
	7	Accounts Payable		500 —	
		Purchases returns and allowances			500 —
		Duke company-missing purchases 4/4			
	9	Sales returns and Allowances		100 —	
		Accounts Receivable			100 —
		Ray Company-return of sales			
	13	Accounts Payable		2500 —	
		Cash			2450 —
		Purchase Discounts			50 —
	16	Cash		495 —	
		Sales Discount		5 —	
		Accounts Receivable			500 —
		Ray Company-Sales of 4/6			
4B.1. Mar	1	Purchases		5000 —	
		Accounts Payable			5000 —
		Purchases from Z company 2/10, n/30			
	1	Accounts Receivable		5000 —	
		Sales			5000 —
		Sales to Y company 2/10, n/3			
	5	Accounts Payable		1000 —	
		Purchase returns and Allowances			1000 —
	5	Sales returns and allowances		1000 —	
		Accounts Receivable			1000
	8	Accounts Payable		4000 —	
		Purchase discount			80
		Cash			3920 —
	8	Cash		3920 —	
		Sale discounts		80 —	
		Accounts Receivable			4000 —

2.

ALLEY COMPANY
Schedule of Cost of Goods Sold
For the Year Ended December 31, 19–

Merchandise Inventory Jan 1, 19--			$30000 —
Purchases		$400000 —	
Less: Purchase returns & Allowances	$2000 —		
Purchase discounts	5000 —	7000 —	
Net Purchases		393000 —	
Plus: Transportation in		10000 —	
Delivered cost of net purchases			403000 —
Cost of goods available for sale			433000 —
Merchandise inventory Dec 31			45000 —
Cost of goods sold			388000 —

Name ______________________

Section ____________ Date ____________

3. **General Journal** *PAGE*

Date		Account Names and Explanations	A/C #	Debit	Credit
19--		a.			
March	5	Accounts Receivable		5000 —	
		Sales 2/10, n/30			5000 —
	15	Cash		4900 —	
		Sales discounts & Returns		100 —	
		Accounts Receivable			5000 —
	30	Cash		5000 —	
		Accounts Receivable			5000 —
		b.			
March	5	Purchases		5000 —	
		Accounts Payable			5000 —
	15	Accounts Payable		5000 —	
		Purchase returns & discounts			100 —
		Cash			4400 —
	30	Accounts Payable		5000 —	
		Cash			5000 —

3000
.02
60.00
4000
.02
80.00

Name ______________ PROBLEM 4.B.6. & ALTERNATE

Section ______________ Date ______________

1) General Journal *PAGE*

Date		Account Names and Explanations	A/C #	Debit	Credit
19--					
May	1	Purchases		3000 —	
		Accounts Payable 2/10, n/30			3000 —
	7	Accounts Payable		3000 —	
		Purchase discounts			60 —
		Cash			2940 —
	10	Purchases		5000 —	
		Accounts Payable 1/10, n/30			5000 —
	11	Accounts Payable		200 —	
		Purchasdiscounts and Allowances			200 —
	14	Accounts Receivable		2000 —	
		Sales 2/10, n/30			2000 —
	25	Accounts Payable		4800 —	
		Cash			4800 —
	27	Cash		2000 —	
		Accounts Receivable			2000 —
	28	Accounts Receivable		4000 —	
		Sales 2/10, n/30			4000 —
	31	Cash		3920 —	
		Sales discounts and Allowances		80 —	
		Accounts Receivable			4000 —

2) **General Journal** *PAGE*

Date		Account Names and Explanations	A/C #	Debit	Credit

Name ____________________ **PROBLEM 4.B.7. & ALTERNATE**

Section ____________ Date ____________

General Journal *PAGE*

Date		Account Names and Explanations	A/C #	Debit	Credit
19--					
June	2	Purchases		3000 —	
		Accounts Payable 2/10, n/30			3000 —
	3	Cash		125 —	
		Sales			125 —
	5	Sales returns and Allowances 6/3		125 —	
		Cash			125 —
	14	Accounts Payable		3000 —	
		Cash			3000 —
	14	Purchases		8000 —	
		Accounts Payable 2/10, n/30			8000 —
	15	Accounts Payable 6/14 purchases		2000 —	
		Purchase returns and Allowances			2000 —
	21	Accounts Payable 6/14		6000 —	
		Cash			6000 —
	24	Accounts Receivable		300 —	
		Sales 1/10, n/30			300 —
	30	Cash		270 —	
		Sales discounts and Allowances		30 —	
		Accounts Receivable			300 —

General Journal *PAGE*

Date		Account Names and Explanations	A/C #	Debit	Credit

Name ______________________

Section ____________ Date ____________

PROBLEM 4.B.8.

1)

General Journal

PAGE

Date		Account Names and Explanations	A/C #	Debit	Credit

2) **General Journal** *PAGE*

Date		Account Names and Explanations	A/C #	Debit	Credit

Name ______________________ PROBLEM 4.B.8. *(Concluded)*

Section ______________ Date ____________

3) General Journal *PAGE*

Date		Account Names and Explanations	A/C #	Debit	Credit
		a)			
		b)			

Name ____________________

Section ____________ Date ____________

PROBLEM 4.B.9.

SMITHFIELD SOAP COMPANY
Schedule of Cost of Goods Sold
For the Year Ended December 31, 19--

Name ______________________ PROBLEM 4.B.10.

Section ____________ Date ____________

1)

CROSSLAND MARKETING COMPANY
Schedule of Cost of Goods Sold
For the Month of November, 19--

2)

CROSSLAND MARKETING COMPANY
Income Statement
For the Month of November, 19--

Name ______________________

Section __________ Date __________

PROBLEM 4.B.11.

1)

2)

3)

Name ______________________________

Section ______________ Date ____________

1. 1) A ten-column work sheet for this requirement can be found at the back of this volume.

2)

DUXAL COMPANY
Income Statement
For the Year Ended September 30, 19X5

3)

DUXAL COMPANY
Balance Sheet
September 30, 19X5

Name ______________________

Section ____________ Date ____________

4) **General Journal** *PAGE*

Date		Account Names and Explanations	A/C #	Debit	Credit

General Journal *PAGE*

Date		Account Names and Explanations	A/C #	Debit	Credit

2.

Name ______________________ **PROBLEM 4.C.4. & ALTERNATE**

Section ____________ Date __________

1) A partially completed ten-column work sheet for this requirement (and a separate partially completed work sheet for Alternate 4.C.4.) can be found at the back of this volume.

2)

____

Income Statement

____

____

Balance Sheet

Name ____________________

Section ____________ Date ____________

1) A ten-column work sheet for this requirement can be found at the back of this volume.

2)

____

Income Statement

____

____

3)

Balance Sheet

Name ______________________

Section ____________ Date ____________

4) **General Journal** *PAGE*

Date		Account Names and Explanations	A/C #	Debit	Credit

General Journal *PAGE*

Date		Account Names and Explanations	A/C #	Debit	Credit

Name ______________________

Section ____________ Date __________

5)

Income Statement

Schedule of Cost of Goods Sold

Name ____________________

Section ____________ Date ____________

PROBLEM 4.C.6. & ALTERNATE

1) A ten-column work sheet for this requirement can be found at the back of this volume.

2) **General Journal** *PAGE*

Date		Account Names and Explanations	A/C #	Debit	Credit

Name ______________________________

Section ______________ Date ______________

PROBLEM 4.C.7.

1)

TRAVIS DISCOUNT STORES
Income Statement
For the Year Ended December 31, 19--

For use by those students who choose to prepare a separate schedule of cost of goods sold to accompany the single-step income statement.

TRAVIS DISCOUNT STORES
Schedule of Cost of Goods Sold
For the Year Ended December 31, 19--

Name ____________________
Section ____________ Date ____________

2)

TRAVIS DISCOUNT STORES
Income Statement
For the Year Ended December 31, 19--

Name ______________________ **PROBLEM 4.C.8.**

Section ____________ Date ____________

1) A partially completed ten-column worksheet for this requirement can be found at the back of this volume.

2)

O'CONNOR STORES
Income Statement
For the Year Ended December 31, 19--

O'CONNOR STORES
Balance Sheet
December 31, 19--

Name ______________________ PROBLEM 4.C.8. *(Concluded)*

Section ______________ Date ______________

3) General Journal *PAGE*

Date		Account Names and Explanations	A/C #	Debit	Credit

Name ______________________________ **PROBLEM 4.C.9.**

Section ______________ Date __________

1)

2)

3)

4)

5) **General Journal** *PAGE*

Date		Account Names and Explanations	A/C #	Debit	Credit

Name ____________________

Section ____________ Date ____________

PROBLEM 4.1. & ALTERNATE

1) and 6)

General Journal

PAGE

Date	Account Names and Explanations	A/C #	Debit	Credit

General Journal

PAGE

Date		Account Names and Explanations	A/C #	Debit	Credit

Name ______________________________ **PROBLEM 4.1. & ALTERNATE** ***(Continued)***

Section ______________ Date ____________

General Journal *PAGE*

Date		Account Names and Explanations	A/C #	Debit	Credit

2) and 6)

Cash *ACCOUNT NO.* **111**

Date	Item	Ref.	Debit	Credit	Balance	
					Debit	*Credit*

Accounts Receivable *ACCOUNT NO.* **112**

Date	Item	Ref.	Debit	Credit	Balance	
					Debit	*Credit*

Merchandise Inventory *ACCOUNT NO.* **113**

Date	Item	Ref.	Debit	Credit	Balance	
					Debit	*Credit*

Name ______________________

Section ____________ Date ____________

Furnishings *ACCOUNT NO.* **116**

Date	Item	Ref.	Debit	Credit	Balance	
					Debit	*Credit*

Accumulated Depreciation—Furnishings *ACCOUNT NO.* **0116**

Date	Item	Ref.	Debit	Credit	Balance	
					Debit	*Credit*

Accounts Payable *ACCOUNT NO.* **211**

Date	Item	Ref.	Debit	Credit	Balance	
					Debit	*Credit*

Wages Payable *ACCOUNT NO.* **212**

Date	Item	Ref.	Debit	Credit	Balance	
					Debit	*Credit*

Notes Payable (due in 2 years) *ACCOUNT NO.* **213**

Date		Item	Ref.	Debit	Credit	Balance	
						Debit	*Credit*

, Capital *ACCOUNT NO.* **311**

Date		Item	Ref.	Debit	Credit	Balance	
						Debit	*Credit*

, Withdrawals *ACCOUNT NO.* **312**

Date		Item	Ref.	Debit	Credit	Balance	
						Debit	*Credit*

Sales *ACCOUNT NO.* **411**

Date		Item	Ref.	Debit	Credit	Balance	
						Debit	*Credit*

Name ____________________

Section __________ Date __________

Sales Discounts *ACCOUNT NO.* 412

Date	Item	Ref.	Debit	Credit	Balance	
					Debit	*Credit*

Sales Returns and Allowances *ACCOUNT NO.* 413

Date	Item	Ref.	Debit	Credit	Balance	
					Debit	*Credit*

Cost of Goods Sold *ACCOUNT NO.* 510

Date	Item	Ref.	Debit	Credit	Balance	
					Debit	*Credit*

Purchases *ACCOUNT NO.* 511

Date	Item	Ref.	Debit	Credit	Balance	
					Debit	*Credit*

Purchases Discounts *ACCOUNT NO.* **512**

Date		Item	Ref.	Debit	Credit	Balance	
						Debit	*Credit*

Purchases Returns and Allowances *ACCOUNT NO.* **513**

Date		Item	Ref.	Debit	Credit	Balance	
						Debit	*Credit*

Transportation In *ACCOUNT NO.* **514**

Date		Item	Ref.	Debit	Credit	Balance	
						Debit	*Credit*

Wage Expense *ACCOUNT NO.* **611**

Date		Item	Ref.	Debit	Credit	Balance	
						Debit	*Credit*

Name ______________________ Section ____________ Date ____________

Depreciation Expense *ACCOUNT NO.* **612**

Date		Item	Ref.	Debit	Credit	Balance	
						Debit	*Credit*

Rent Expense *ACCOUNT NO.* **613**

Date		Item	Ref.	Debit	Credit	Balance	
						Debit	*Credit*

3) A ten-column work sheet for this requirement can be found at the back of this volume.

4)

Income Statement

Name ______________________ **PROBLEM 4.1. & ALTERNATE** ***(Concluded)***

Section ____________ Date ____________

5)

Balance Sheet

Name ____________________

Section ____________ Date ____________

PROBLEM 4.2. & ALTERNATE

1) and 6) **General Journal** *PAGE*

Date		Account Names and Explanations	A/C #	Debit	Credit

General Journal *PAGE*

Date		Account Names and Explanations	A/C #	Debit	Credit

Name ____________________

Section ______________ Date ______________

PROBLEM 4.2. & ALTERNATE *(Continued)*

General Journal *PAGE*

Date		Account Names and Explanations	A/C #	Debit	Credit

2) and 6)

Cash *ACCOUNT NO.* 11

Date	Item	Ref.	Debit	Credit	Balance	
					Debit	*Credit*

Accounts Receivable *ACCOUNT NO.* 12

Date	Item	Ref.	Debit	Credit	Balance	
					Debit	*Credit*

Merchandise Inventory *ACCOUNT NO.* 13

Date	Item	Ref.	Debit	Credit	Balance	
					Debit	*Credit*

Name ____________________ **PROBLEM 4.2. & ALTERNATE** ***(Continued)***

Section __________ Date __________

Furniture and Fixtures *ACCOUNT NO.* **15**

Date	Item	Ref.	Debit	Credit	Balance	
					Debit	*Credit*

Accum. Depr.—Furniture and Fixtures *ACCOUNT NO.* **015**

Date	Item	Ref.	Debit	Credit	Balance	
					Debit	*Credit*

Accounts Payable *ACCOUNT NO.* **21**

Date	Item	Ref.	Debit	Credit	Balance	
					Debit	*Credit*

Salaries Payable *ACCOUNT NO.* **22**

Date	Item	Ref.	Debit	Credit	Balance	
					Debit	*Credit*

Interest Payable *ACCOUNT NO.* 23

Date		Item	Ref.	Debit	Credit	Balance	
						Debit	*Credit*

Loan Payable (due in 3 years) *ACCOUNT NO.* 24

Date		Item	Ref.	Debit	Credit	Balance	
						Debit	*Credit*

, Capital *ACCOUNT NO.* 31

Date		Item	Ref.	Debit	Credit	Balance	
						Debit	*Credit*

, Withdrawals *ACCOUNT NO.* 32

Date		Item	Ref.	Debit	Credit	Balance	
						Debit	*Credit*

Name ____________________

Section __________ Date __________

Sales — *ACCOUNT NO.* 41

Date	Item	Ref.	Debit	Credit	Balance	
					Debit	*Credit*

Sales Discounts — *ACCOUNT NO.* 42

Date	Item	Ref.	Debit	Credit	Balance	
					Debit	*Credit*

Sales Returns and Allowances — *ACCOUNT NO.* 43

Date	Item	Ref.	Debit	Credit	Balance	
					Debit	*Credit*

Cost of Goods Sold — *ACCOUNT NO.* 51

Date	Item	Ref.	Debit	Credit	Balance	
					Debit	*Credit*

Purchases *ACCOUNT NO.* 52

Date	Item	Ref.	Debit	Credit	Balance	
					Debit	*Credit*

Purchases Discounts *ACCOUNT NO.* 53

Date	Item	Ref.	Debit	Credit	Balance	
					Debit	*Credit*

Purchases Returns and Allowances *ACCOUNT NO.* 54

Date	Item	Ref.	Debit	Credit	Balance	
					Debit	*Credit*

Freight In *ACCOUNT NO.* 55

Date	Item	Ref.	Debit	Credit	Balance	
					Debit	*Credit*

Salary Expense *ACCOUNT NO.* 61

Date		Item	Ref.	Debit	Credit	Balance	
						Debit	*Credit*

Rent Expense *ACCOUNT NO.* 62

Date		Item	Ref.	Debit	Credit	Balance	
						Debit	*Credit*

Depreciation Expense *ACCOUNT NO.* 63

Date		Item	Ref.	Debit	Credit	Balance	
						Debit	*Credit*

Interest Expense *ACCOUNT NO.* 64

Date		Item	Ref.	Debit	Credit	Balance	
						Debit	*Credit*

3) A ten-column worksheet for this requirement can be found at the back of this volume.

4)

Income Statement

Name ______________________

Section ____________ Date ____________

5)

Balance Sheet

Name ______________________________

Section ______________ Date __________

COMPREHENSION PROBLEM 4.3.

1)

2)

3)

Name

Section Date

COMPREHENSION PROBLEM 4.4.

1)

2)

3)

Name ______________________________

Section ____________ Date ____________

COMPREHENSION PROBLEM 4.5.

1)

General Journal

PAGE

Date		Account Names and Explanations	A/C #	Debit	Credit

2) **General Journal** *PAGE*

Date		Account Names and Explanations	A/C #	Debit	Credit

Name ______________________

Section ____________ Date ____________

1. Subsidiary ledgers are accounts subdividing a general ledger.

2. 1) and 3)

SALES JOURNAL FOR THE MONTH OF September, 19--

PAGE S16

Date		Customer	Invoice Number	Ref.	Accounts Receivable *Debit*	Sales Tax Payable *Credit*	Sales *Credit*
Sept.	30	Brought Forward			18411 96	876 76	17535 20
	30	Alan Wahoo	1435		200 —	10 —	17725 20

CASH RECEIPTS JOURNAL FOR THE MONTH OF September, 19– *PAGE* CR25

Date		Accounts and Explanations	Ref.	General Debit	General Credit	Accounts Receivable Credit	Sales Credit	Sales Tax Payable Credit	Cash Debit
Sept.	30	Brought Forward		85 00	1 000 00	1 675 040	45 218 60	2 260 90	65 144 90
	30	Archie Ball on account				150 —			

Name ____________________

Section ____________ Date ____________

2) **ACCOUNTS RECEIVABLE SUBSIDIARY LEDGER**

NAME Archie Ball

ADDRESS 1436 Tee Street, Tarrytown, NY 10591

Date		Item	Ref.	Debit	Credit	Balance
19–						
Sept.	20		S15	150 00		150 00

NAME Alan Wahoo

ADDRESS 3285 Bee Street, Tarrytown, NY 10591

Date		Item	Ref.	Debit	Credit	Balance
19–						
Sept.	1	Balance	X			240 00
	10		CR24		240 00	-0-

4) **GENERAL LEDGER**

Accounts Receivable *ACCOUNT NO.* **114**

Date		Item	Ref.	Debit	Credit	Balance	
						Debit	*Credit*
19–							
Sept.	1	Balance	X			8460 75	

Sales *ACCOUNT NO.* **411**

Date		Item	Ref.	Debit	Credit	Balance	
						Debit	*Credit*

3.

NELLY COMPANY
Schedule of Accounts Receivable
September 30, 19--

Name ______________________________ **PROBLEM 5.A.4. & ALTERNATE**

Section ______________ Date ____________

1) and 2)

SALES JOURNAL FOR THE MONTH OF ______________________________ *PAGE* ________

Date		**Customer**	**Invoice Number**	**Ref.**	**Accounts Receivable**	**Sales Tax Payable**	**Sales**
					Debit	*Credit*	*Credit*

5A1

CASH RECEIPTS JOURNAL FOR THE MONTH OF ______________ *PAGE* ______

Date		Accounts and Explanations	Ref.	General Debit	General Credit	Accounts Receivable Credit	Sales Credit	Sales Tax Payable Credit	Cash Debit
Oct	2	A. Summers				250 —			250 —
	2	Cash Sales					700 —	42 —	742 —
	3	Note Payable			5000 —				5000 —

Name ____________________

Section ____________ Date ____________

3) ACCOUNTS RECEIVABLE SUBSIDIARY LEDGER

NAME ____________________

ADDRESS ____________________

Date		Item	Ref.	Debit	Credit	Balance

NAME ____________________

ADDRESS ____________________

Date		Item	Ref.	Debit	Credit	Balance

NAME ____________________

ADDRESS ____________________

Date		Item	Ref.	Debit	Credit	Balance

NAME ______________________________

ADDRESS ______________________________

Date		Item	Ref.	Debit	Credit	Balance

NAME ______________________________

ADDRESS ______________________________

Date		Item	Ref.	Debit	Credit	Balance

NAME ______________________________

ADDRESS ______________________________

Date		Item	Ref.	Debit	Credit	Balance

Name ____________________

Section __________ Date __________

PROBLEM 5.A.4. & ALTERNATE *(Continued)*

4)

GENERAL LEDGER

Cash

ACCOUNT NO. 111

Date		Item	Ref.	Debit	Credit	Balance	
						Debit	*Credit*

Accounts Receivable

ACCOUNT NO. 112

Date		Item	Ref.	Debit	Credit	Balance	
						Debit	*Credit*

Sales Tax Payable

ACCOUNT NO. 213

Date		Item	Ref.	Debit	Credit	Balance	
						Debit	*Credit*

, Capital

ACCOUNT NO. 311

Date		Item	Ref.	Debit	Credit	Balance	
						Debit	*Credit*

Sales *ACCOUNT NO.* **411**

Date		Item	Ref.	Debit	Credit	Balance	
						Debit	*Credit*

5)

Schedule of Accounts Receivable

Name ______________________ **PROBLEM 5.A.5. & ALTERNATE**

Section ______________ Date ____________

1) For Problem 5.A.5.

SALES JOURNAL FOR THE MONTH OF March, 19– *PAGE* S8

Date		Customer	Invoice Number	Ref.	Accounts Receivable *Debit*	Sales Tax Payable *Credit*	Sales *Credit*
Mar.	28	Brought Forward			8652	252	8400
	30	M. Fortz	111	√	206	6	200
	31	J. Fonze	112	√	412	12	400

1) For Alternate 5.A.5.

SALES JOURNAL FOR THE MONTH OF March, 19– *PAGE* S5

Date		Customer	Invoice Number	Ref.	Accounts Receivable *Debit*	Sales Tax Payable *Credit*	Sales *Credit*
Mar.	28	Brought Forward			7230	210	7020
	30	L. Bender	511	√	360	10	350
	31	J. Gwin	512	√	541	15	526

For Problem 5.A.5.

CASH RECEIPTS JOURNAL FOR THE MONTH OF March, 19– *PAGE* CR13

Date		Accounts and Explanations	Ref.	General Debit	General Credit	Accounts Receivable Credit	Sales Credit	Sales Tax Payable Credit	Cash Debit
Mar.	31	Brought Forward		400	3800	8750	12100	363	24613
	31	R. Beckwith	√			800			800

For Alternate 5.A.5.

CASH RECEIPTS JOURNAL FOR THE MONTH OF March, 19– *PAGE* CR18

Date		Accounts and Explanations	Ref.	General Debit	General Credit	Accounts Receivable Credit	Sales Credit	Sales Tax Payable Credit	Cash Debit
Mar.	31	Brought Forward		600	4200	6275	14200	275	24350
	31	B. Roberts	√			750			750

Name ______________________

Section ____________ Date __________

PROBLEM 5.A.5. & ALTERNATE ***(Concluded)***

2)

Cash *ACCOUNT NO.* **111**

Date		Item	Ref.	Debit	Credit	Balance	
						Debit	*Credit*

Accounts Receivable *ACCOUNT NO.* **112**

Date		Item	Ref.	Debit	Credit	Balance	
						Debit	*Credit*

Sales Tax Payable *ACCOUNT NO.* **212**

Date		Item	Ref.	Debit	Credit	Balance	
						Debit	*Credit*

Sales *ACCOUNT NO.* **411**

Date		Item	Ref.	Debit	Credit	Balance	
						Debit	*Credit*

Accounts Receivable 103

Jan1 129000	Jan31 CR3 104,000
S3 88,130	

Sales 601

	1/31 S3 88,130

Dan Arno

1/1 250	1/5 CR1 250
1/30 J102 500	

Mary Bard

1/30 J103 450	

Jeff Car

1/25 S2 40	
1/31 J104 80	

Name ______________________ **PROBLEM 5.A.6. & ALTERNATE**

Section ____________ Date ____________

1) and 3)

SALES JOURNAL FOR THE MONTH OF ______________________ *PAGE* ________

5A2

Date		Customer	Invoice Number	Ref.	Accounts Receivable *Debit*	Sales Tax Payable *Credit*	Sales *Credit*
Jan	3	H. Dinger	1286		530 —	30 —	500 —
	4	B. Gott	1287		636 —	36 —	600 —
	4	K. Carnal	1288		106 —	6 —	100 —

CASH RECEIPTS JOURNAL FOR THE MONTH OF ________________ *PAGE* ______

Date	Accounts and Explanations	Ref.	General		Accounts Receivable	Sales	Sales Tax Payable	Cash
			Debit	*Credit*	*Credit*	*Credit*	*Credit*	*Debit*

Name ______________________

Section ____________ Date ____________

2) **ACCOUNTS RECEIVABLE SUBSIDIARY LEDGER**

NAME ______________________

ADDRESS ______________________

Date		Item	Ref.	Debit	Credit	Balance

NAME ______________________

ADDRESS ______________________

Date		Item	Ref.	Debit	Credit	Balance

4) **GENERAL LEDGER**

Accounts Receivable *ACCOUNT NO.* **112**

Date		Item	Ref.	Debit	Credit	Balance	
						Debit	*Credit*

Sales *ACCOUNT NO.* **411**

Date		Item	Ref.	Debit	Credit	Balance	
						Debit	*Credit*

Name ____________________

Section __________ Date __________

1. 1) and 3)

PURCHASES JOURNAL FOR THE MONTH OF January, 19– *PAGE* P2

Date		Creditor	P. O. No.	Invoice Date	Terms	Ref.	Amount
		Brought Forward					20765
Jan.	30	Varco, Inc.	1361	1/28/–	n/30	√	620

CASH PAYMENTS JOURNAL FOR THE MONTH OF January, 19– *PAGE* CP2

Date		Accounts and Explanations	Ck. No.	Ref.	General Debit	General Credit	Freight In Debit	Accounts Payable Debit	Purchases Discounts Credit	Cash Credit
		Brought Forward			6542	2000		18600	204	22938
Jan.	31	Wage Expense	2831	612	2400					2400

Name ______________________

Section ____________ Date ____________

2) **ACCOUNTS PAYABLE SUBSIDIARY LEDGER**

NAME Art Supply Company

ADDRESS 210 First Street, Clarion, PA 16214

Date		Item	Ref.	Debit	Credit	Balance

NAME Jazzy Corporation

ADDRESS 2114 Fifth Avenue, Knox, PA 16232

Date		Item	Ref.	Debit	Credit	Balance
19–						
Jan.	23		P1		600	600

4) and 5) **GENERAL LEDGER**

Accounts Payable *ACCOUNT NO.* 211

Date		Item	Ref.	Debit	Credit	Balance	
						Debit	*Credit*
19–							
Jan.	1	Balance	X				10400

Purchases *ACCOUNT NO.* 511

Date		Item	Ref.	Debit	Credit	Balance	
						Debit	*Credit*

2. a.

b.

Name ______________________ PROBLEM 5.B.4. & ALTERNATE

Section __________ Date __________

1) and 2)

PURCHASES JOURNAL FOR THE MONTH OF ______________________ *PAGE* ______

Date	Creditor	P. O. No.	Invoice Date	Terms	Ref.	Amount

CASH PAYMENTS JOURNAL FOR THE MONTH OF ______________ *PAGE* ______

5B1

Date		Accounts and Explanations	Ck. No.	Ref.	General Debit	General Credit	Freight In Debit	Accounts Payable Debit	Purchases Discounts Credit	Cash Credit
July	2	Equipment	448		1200—					1200—
	5	Super Freight Lines	449				48—			48—
	8	Krackoff Company	450					1000—	20—	980—
	15	Salary Expense	451		750—					750—

Name ______________________________ PROBLEM 5.B.4. & ALTERNATE *(Continued)*

Section ______________ Date ___________

3) ACCOUNTS PAYABLE SUBSIDIARY LEDGER

NAME ______________________________

ADDRESS ______________________________

Date		Item	Ref.	Debit	Credit	Balance

NAME ______________________________

ADDRESS ______________________________

Date		Item	Ref.	Debit	Credit	Balance

NAME ______________________________

ADDRESS ______________________________

Date		Item	Ref.	Debit	Credit	Balance

NAME ______________________________

ADDRESS ______________________________

Date		Item	Ref.	Debit	Credit	Balance

4)

GENERAL LEDGER

Cash *ACCOUNT NO.* **111**

Date	Item	Ref.	Debit	Credit	Balance	
					Debit	*Credit*

Accounts Payable *ACCOUNT NO.* **201**

Date	Item	Ref.	Debit	Credit	Balance	
					Debit	*Credit*

, Withdrawals *ACCOUNT NO.* **302**

Date	Item	Ref.	Debit	Credit	Balance	
					Debit	*Credit*

Purchases *ACCOUNT NO.* **501**

Date	Item	Ref.	Debit	Credit	Balance	
					Debit	*Credit*

Purchases Discounts *ACCOUNT NO.* **502**

Date	Item	Ref.	Debit	Credit	Balance	
					Debit	*Credit*

Wages *ACCOUNT NO.* **604**

Date	Item	Ref.	Debit	Credit	Balance	
					Debit	*Credit*

Building Rent *ACCOUNT NO.* **608**

Date	Item	Ref.	Debit	Credit	Balance	
					Debit	*Credit*

5)

Schedule of Accounts Payable

Name ______________________________ **PROBLEM 5.B.5. & ALTERNATE**

Section ______________ Date ______________

1) and 2) **For Problem 5.B.5.**

PURCHASES JOURNAL FOR THE MONTH OF May, 19-- *PAGE* P18

Date		Creditor	P. O. No.	Invoice Date	Terms	Ref.	Amount
		Brought Forward					405 00
May	31	Barfeo, Inc.	PO867	5/26	1/10, n/30	√	3 00

For Alternate 5.B.5.

PURCHASES JOURNAL FOR THE MONTH OF July, 19-- *PAGE* P28

Date		Creditor	P. O. No.	Invoice Date	Terms	Ref.	Amount
		Brought Forward					317 50
July	30	Polce Company	PO742	7/20	2/10, n/30		4 90

For Problem 5.B.5.

CASH PAYMENTS JOURNAL FOR THE MONTH OF May, 19--

PAGE CP21

Date		Accounts and Explanations	Ck. No.	Ref.	General		Freight In	Accounts Payable	Purchases Discounts	Cash
					Debit	*Credit*	*Debit*	*Debit*	*Credit*	*Credit*
		Brought Forward			7500	3700	480	31000	640	34640
May	29	Office Supplies	3006	115	80					80

For Alternate 5.B.5.

CASH PAYMENTS JOURNAL FOR THE MONTH OF July, 19--

PAGE CP23

Date		Accounts and Explanations	Ck. No.	Ref.	General		Freight In	Accounts Payable	Purchases Discounts	Cash
					Debit	*Credit*	*Debit*	*Debit*	*Credit*	*Credit*
		Brought Forward			8750	2950	520	42000	780	47540
July	19	Office Supplies	2467	115	95					95

Name ______________________

Section ____________ Date ____________

3)

GENERAL LEDGER

Accounts Payable *ACCOUNT NO.* 211

Date	Item	Ref.	Debit	Credit	Balance Debit	Balance Credit

Purchases *ACCOUNT NO.* 511

Date	Item	Ref.	Debit	Credit	Balance Debit	Balance Credit

ACCOUNTS PAYABLE SUBSIDIARY LEDGER

NAME ______________________

ADDRESS ______________________

Date	Item	Ref.	Debit	Credit	Balance

NAME ______________________

ADDRESS ______________________

Date	Item	Ref.	Debit	Credit	Balance

Name ____________________

Section ____________ Date ____________

PROBLEM 5.B.6. & ALTERNATE

1) For Problem 5.B.6.

CASH PAYMENTS JOURNAL FOR THE MONTH OF February, 19--

PAGE CP28

Date		Accounts and Explanations	Ck. No.	Ref.	General Debit	General Credit	Freight In Debit	Accounts Payable Debit	Purchases Discounts Credit	Cash Credit
		Brought Forward			10000	8040	80	12000	70	13970
Feb.	27	Meeter Company	0133					980	20	980
	27	Equipment	0134		4000					
	28	Harkwell, Inc.	0135					1200		1200

For Alternate 5.B.6.

CASH PAYMENTS JOURNAL FOR THE MONTH OF October, 19--

PAGE CP30

Date		Accounts and Explanations	Ck. No.	Ref.	General Debit	General Credit	Freight In Debit	Accounts Payable Debit	Purchases Discounts Credit	Cash Credit
		Brought Forward			25000	7350	95	13200	80	30865
Oct.	20	Williams, Inc.	0147					720	14	720
	25	Equipment	0148		2500					
	28	Sample Company	0149					1570		1570

2)

GENERAL LEDGER

Cash

ACCOUNT NO. 111

Date		Item	Ref.	Debit	Credit	Balance	
						Debit	*Credit*

Equipment

ACCOUNT NO. 116

Date		Item	Ref.	Debit	Credit	Balance	
						Debit	*Credit*

Accounts Payable

ACCOUNT NO. 211

Date		Item	Ref.	Debit	Credit	Balance	
						Debit	*Credit*

Purchases Discounts

ACCOUNT NO. 513

Date		Item	Ref.	Debit	Credit	Balance	
						Debit	*Credit*

Name ______________________

Section ____________ Date ____________

PROBLEM 5.B.6. & ALTERNATE *(Concluded)*

Freight In

ACCOUNT NO. 514

Date	Item	Ref.	Debit	Credit	Balance	
					Debit	*Credit*

ACCOUNTS PAYABLE SUBSIDIARY LEDGER

NAME ______________________

ADDRESS ______________________

Date	Item	Ref.	Debit	Credit	Balance

NAME ______________________

ADDRESS ______________________

Date	Item	Ref.	Debit	Credit	Balance

AP 201

1/31 CP3 35,000	1/1 Bal. 90,000
	31 P3 72,400

Purchases 701

1/31 P3 72,400	

Danny's Doodad's

1/15 CP2 4,000	1/5 P1 4,000
	30 P3 1,200

Jeanie's Clothiers

	1/31 P3 2,700

Name ______________________

Section ____________ Date ____________

PROBLEM 5.B.7.

PURCHASES JOURNAL FOR THE MONTH OF March, 19-- *PAGE* P8

Date		Creditor	P. O. No.	Invoice Date	Terms	Ref.	Amount
Mar.	3	Great Company	611	2/28	n/30		1500
	8	Zebox, Inc.	590	3/6	1/10, n/30		2000
	11	Great Company	613	3/10	n/30		800
	12	Aaron Supply	620	3/10	n/30		400
	18	Hearfelt, Inc.	610	3/15	2/10, n/30		3000
	25	Zebox, Inc.	621	3/22	1/10, n/30		1500
	25	Great Company	622	3/23	n/30		2100
	30	Great Company	612	3/28	n/30		600
	31	Aaron Supply	614	3/30	n/10		1400
							13300
5B2 Apr	8	Keper Corporation	616	4/5	1/10, n/30		800 —
	12	Filmax Company	598	4/10	n/10		1000 —
	21	Hardy Inc	621	4/16	2/10, n/30		11000 —

GENERAL LEDGER

Accounts Payable — *ACCOUNT NO.* 211

Date		Item	Ref.	Debit	Credit	Balance Debit	Balance Credit
19–							
Mar.	1	Balance	X				12500

Purchases — *ACCOUNT NO.* 512

Date		Item	Ref.	Debit	Credit	Balance Debit	Balance Credit

ACCOUNTS PAYABLE SUBSIDIARY LEDGER

NAME Aaron Supply

ADDRESS

Date		Item	Ref.	Debit	Credit	Balance
19–						
Mar.	1	Balance	X			900

NAME Great Company

ADDRESS

Date		Item	Ref.	Debit	Credit	Balance
19–						
Mar.	1	Balance	X			1300

Name ______________________________
Section ______________ Date __________

PROBLEM 5.B.7. ***(Concluded)***

NAME Hearfelt, Inc.
ADDRESS ______________________________

Date		Item	Ref.	Debit	Credit	Balance

NAME Zebox, Inc.
ADDRESS ______________________________

Date		Item	Ref.	Debit	Credit	Balance

Name ______________________

Section __________ Date __________

1) and 2) For Problem 5.1.

PURCHASES JOURNAL FOR THE MONTH OF June, 19–   *PAGE* P18

Date		Creditor	P. O. No.	Invoice Date	Terms	Ref.	Amount
		Brought Forward					382 00
June	27	Frame Company	PO28	6/25	1/10, n/30	√	5 00

For Alternate 5.1.

PURCHASES JOURNAL FOR THE MONTH OF February, 19–   *PAGE* P20

Date		Creditor	P. O. No.	Invoice Date	Terms	Ref.	Amount
		Brought Forward					198 00
Feb.	22	Gluck Corporation	PO46	2/20	2/10, n/30	√	4 00

For Problem 5.1.

SALES JOURNAL FOR THE MONTH OF June, 19-- *PAGE* S24

Date		Customer	Invoice Number	Ref.	Accounts Receivable Debit	Sales Tax Payable Credit	Sales Credit
		Brought Forward			42930	2430	40500
June	28	Hintzen, Inc.	1285	√	848	48	800

For Alternate 5.1.

SALES JOURNAL FOR THE MONTH OF February, 19-- *PAGE* S19

Date		Customer	Invoice Number	Ref.	Accounts Receivable Debit	Sales Tax Payable Credit	Sales Credit
		Brought Forward			64850	3850	61000
Feb.	20	M. Parde	4626	√	963	63	900

Name ____________________

Section ____________ Date ____________

For Problem 5.1.

CASH PAYMENTS JOURNAL FOR THE MONTH OF June, 19–

PAGE CP20

Date	Accounts and Explanations	Ck. No.	Ref.	General Debit	General Credit	Freight In Debit	Accounts Payable Debit	Purchases Discounts Credit	Cash Credit
	Brought Forward			68 00	26 00	3 90	326 00	5 50	366 40

For Alternate 5.1.

CASH PAYMENTS JOURNAL FOR THE MONTH OF February, 19–

PAGE CP13

Date	Accounts and Explanations	Ck. No.	Ref.	General Debit	General Credit	Freight In Debit	Accounts Payable Debit	Purchases Discounts Credit	Cash Credit
	Brought Forward			7 50	32 00	6 50	274 00	4 80	251 20

For Problem 5.1.

CASH RECEIPTS JOURNAL FOR THE MONTH OF June, 19--

PAGE CR31

Date	Accounts and Explanations	Ref.	General Debit	General Credit	Accounts Receivable Credit	Sales Credit	Sales Tax Payable Credit	Cash Debit
	Brought Forward		5060	3900	11900	16000	840	27580

For Alternate 5.1.

CASH RECEIPTS JOURNAL FOR THE MONTH OF February, 19--

PAGE CR21

Date	Accounts and Explanations	Ref.	General Debit	General Credit	Accounts Receivable Credit	Sales Credit	Sales Tax Payable Credit	Cash Debit
	Brought Forward		6100	7000	8700	21400	1260	32260

Name ____________________

Section ____________ Date ____________

3)

GENERAL LEDGER

Cash

ACCOUNT NO. 111

Date		Item	Ref.	Debit	Credit	Balance	
						Debit	*Credit*

Accounts Receivable

ACCOUNT NO. 112

Date		Item	Ref.	Debit	Credit	Balance	
						Debit	*Credit*

Accounts Payable

ACCOUNT NO. 211

Date		Item	Ref.	Debit	Credit	Balance	
						Debit	*Credit*

Sales

ACCOUNT NO. 411

Date		Item	Ref.	Debit	Credit	Balance	
						Debit	*Credit*

SUBSIDIARY LEDGERS

Accounts Receivable Ledger

NAME ______________________________

ADDRESS ______________________________

Date		Item	Ref.	Debit	Credit	Balance

NAME ______________________________

ADDRESS ______________________________

Date		Item	Ref.	Debit	Credit	Balance

Name ______________________

Section ____________ Date ____________

Accounts Payable Ledger

NAME ______________________

ADDRESS ______________________

Date		Item	Ref.	Debit	Credit	Balance

NAME ______________________

ADDRESS ______________________

Date		Item	Ref.	Debit	Credit	Balance

Name
Section Date

1) and 2)

PURCHASES JOURNAL FOR THE MONTH OF April, 19-- *PAGE* P20

Date		Creditor	P. O. No.	Invoice Date	Terms	Ref.	Amount
		Brought Forward					238 00

SALES JOURNAL FOR THE MONTH OF April, 19-- *PAGE* S22

Date		Customer	Invoice Number	Ref.	Accounts Receivable *Debit*	Sales Tax Payable *Credit*	Sales *Credit*
		Brought Forward			477 00	27 00	450 00

CASH PAYMENTS JOURNAL FOR THE MONTH OF April, 19–

PAGE CP12

Date	Accounts And Explanations	Ck. No.	Ref.	General Debit	General Credit	Freight In Debit	Accounts Payable Debit	Purchases Discounts Credit	Cash Credit
	Brought Forward			9500	1400	700	21100	450	29450

CASH RECEIPTS JOURNAL FOR THE MONTH OF April, 19–

PAGE CR16

Date	Accounts and Explanations	Ref.	General Debit	General Credit	Accounts Receivable Credit	Sales Credit	Sales Tax Payable Credit	Cash Debit
	Brought Forward		-0-	-0-	21600	8200	492	30292

Name ______________________________ PROBLEM 5.2. & ALTERNATE *(Continued)*

Section ______________ Date ____________

3), 5) and 11)

GENERAL LEDGER

Cash

ACCOUNT NO. **111**

Date		Item	Ref.	Debit	Credit	Balance Debit	Balance Credit
19–							
Apr.	1	Balance	X			6100	

Accounts Receivable

ACCOUNT NO. **112**

Date		Item	Ref.	Debit	Credit	Balance Debit	Balance Credit
19–							
Apr.	1	Balance	X			26350	

Merchandise Inventory

ACCOUNT NO. **113**

Date		Item	Ref.	Debit	Credit	Balance Debit	Balance Credit
19–							
Apr.	1	Balance	X			42000	

Equipment

ACCOUNT NO. **116**

Date		Item	Ref.	Debit	Credit	Balance Debit	Balance Credit
19–							
Apr.	1	Balance	X			11000	

Accumulated Depreciation—Equipment *ACCOUNT NO.* **0116**

Date		Item	Ref.	Debit	Credit	Balance Debit	Balance Credit
19–							
Apr.	1	Balance	X				4000

Accounts Payable *ACCOUNT NO.* **211**

Date		Item	Ref.	Debit	Credit	Balance Debit	Balance Credit
19–							
Apr.	1	Balance	X				27000

Sales Tax Payable *ACCOUNT NO.* **212**

Date		Item	Ref.	Debit	Credit	Balance Debit	Balance Credit
19–							
Apr.	1	Balance	X				200

Bank Loan Payable (due in 3 years) *ACCOUNT NO.* **215**

Date		Item	Ref.	Debit	Credit	Balance Debit	Balance Credit
19–							
Apr.	1	Balance	X				10000

Name ____________________ **PROBLEM 5.2. & ALTERNATE *(Continued)***

Section ____________ Date __________

Interest Payable *ACCOUNT NO.* 216

Date		Item	Ref.	Debit	Credit	Balance Debit	Balance Credit
19–							
Apr.	1	Balance	X				250

S. Case, Capital *ACCOUNT NO.* 311

Date		Item	Ref.	Debit	Credit	Balance Debit	Balance Credit
19–							
Apr.	1	Balance	X				44000

S. Case, Withdrawals *ACCOUNT NO.* 312

Date		Item	Ref.	Debit	Credit	Balance Debit	Balance Credit

Sales *ACCOUNT NO.* 411

Date		Item	Ref.	Debit	Credit	Balance Debit	Balance Credit

Purchases — *ACCOUNT NO.* 511

Date		Item	Ref.	Debit	Credit	Balance	
						Debit	*Credit*

Freight In — *ACCOUNT NO.* 512

Date		Item	Ref.	Debit	Credit	Balance	
						Debit	*Credit*

Purchases Discounts — *ACCOUNT NO.* 513

Date		Item	Ref.	Debit	Credit	Balance	
						Debit	*Credit*

Cost of Goods Sold — *ACCOUNT NO.* 611

Date		Item	Ref.	Debit	Credit	Balance	
						Debit	*Credit*

Name ________________________

Section ____________ Date ____________

PROBLEM 5.2. & ALTERNATE ***(Continued)***

Wage Expense *ACCOUNT NO.* **612**

Date		Item	Ref.	Debit	Credit	Balance	
						Debit	*Credit*

Rent Expense *ACCOUNT NO.* **613**

Date		Item	Ref.	Debit	Credit	Balance	
						Debit	*Credit*

Advertising Expense *ACCOUNT NO.* **614**

Date		Item	Ref.	Debit	Credit	Balance	
						Debit	*Credit*

Utilities Expense *ACCOUNT NO.* **615**

Date		Item	Ref.	Debit	Credit	Balance	
						Debit	*Credit*

Depreciation Expense *ACCOUNT NO.* **616**

Date		Item	Ref.	Debit	Credit	Balance	
						Debit	*Credit*

Interest Expense *ACCOUNT NO.* **617**

Date		Item	Ref.	Debit	Credit	Balance	
						Debit	*Credit*

4) and 5) **ACCOUNTS RECEIVABLE LEDGER ACCOUNT**

NAME B. Quano

ADDRESS ______

Date		Item	Ref.	Debit	Credit	Balance

Name ______________________

Section ____________ Date __________

ACCOUNTS PAYABLE LEDGER ACCOUNTS

NAME Ace Wholesale

ADDRESS ______________________

Date		Item	Ref.	Debit	Credit	Balance

NAME Alex Company

ADDRESS ______________________

Date		Item	Ref.	Debit	Credit	Balance

6) A ten-column work sheet for this requirement can be found at the back of this volume.

7)

CASE COMPANY
Schedule of Accounts Receivable
April 30, 19--

CASE COMPANY
Schedule of Accounts Payable
April 30, 19--

Name ______________________

Section ______________ Date ____________

8)

CASE COMPANY
Income Statement
For the Month Ended April 30, 19--

9)

CASE COMPANY
Balance Sheet
April 30, 19--

Name ____________________ PROBLEM 5.2. & ALTERNATE *(Continued)*

Section ____________ Date ____________

10) **General Journal** *PAGE* 8

Date		Account Names and Explanations	A/C #	Debit	Credit

General Journal

PAGE 9

Date		Account Names and Explanations	A/C #	Debit	Credit

PROBLEM 5.3. & ALTERNATE

Name ____________________

Section __________ Date __________

1) and 2)

CASH PAYMENTS JOURNAL FOR THE MONTH OF ____________________ *PAGE* ______

Date	Accounts and Explanations	Ck. No.	Ref.	General		Freight In	Accounts Payable	Purchases Discounts	Cash
				Debit	*Credit*	*Debit*	*Debit*	*Credit*	*Credit*

CASH RECEIPTS JOURNAL FOR THE MONTH OF ______________________ *PAGE* ________

Date	Accounts and Explanations	Ref.	General		Accounts Receivable	Sales	Sales Tax Payable	Cash
			Debit	*Credit*	*Credit*	*Credit*	*Credit*	*Debit*

Name ____________________ PROBLEM 5.3. & ALTERNATE *(Continued)*

Section ____________ Date ____________

3) GENERAL LEDGER ACCOUNTS

Cash ACCOUNT NO. 111

Date		Item	Ref.	Debit	Credit	Balance	
						Debit	*Credit*

Accounts Receivable ACCOUNT NO. 112

Date		Item	Ref.	Debit	Credit	Balance	
						Debit	*Credit*

Notes Payable ACCOUNT NO. 212

Date		Item	Ref.	Debit	Credit	Balance	
						Debit	*Credit*

ACCOUNTS RECEIVABLE LEDGER ACCOUNTS

NAME ______________________

ADDRESS ______________________ *ACCOUNT NO.*

Date		Item	Ref.	Debit	Credit	Balance

NAME ______________________

ADDRESS ______________________ *ACCOUNT NO.*

Date		Item	Ref.	Debit	Credit	Balance

Name ______________________

Section ____________ Date ________

1)

COMPREHENSION PROBLEM 5.4. *(Continued)*

2)

Name ______________________

Section ______________ Date __________

3)

4)

5)

Name ____________________ **SELF-QUIZ FOR SECTION 6.A**

Section __________ Date __________

1. **General Journal** *PAGE*

Date		Account Names and Explanations	A/C #	Debit	Credit
		a. Darling Company			
19--					
Dec	1	Notes Receivable		4000 —	
		Accounts Receivable—Blake Co.			4000 —
		60 at 9% interest			
	31	Interest Receivable		30 —	
		Interest Revenue			30 —
Jan	30	Cash		4060 —	
		Notes Receivable			4000 —
		Accrued Interest Receivable			30 —
		Interest Payable			30 —
19--		b. Blake Company			
Dec	1	Accounts Payable		4000 —	
		Notes Payable			4000 —
		60 days at 9% interest			
	31	Interest Expense		30 —	
		Interest Payable			30 —
Jan	30	Notes Payable		4000 —	
		Interest Payable		30 —	
		Interest Expense		30 —	
		Cash			4060 —

2. General Journal PAGE

Date		Account Names and Explanations	A/C #	Debit	Credit
19--					
Dec	1	Notes Receivable		6000 —	
		Accounts Receivable			6000 —
		90 day at 12% int.			
	31	Interest Receivable		60 —	
		Interest Revenue			60 —
March	1	Cash			
		Notes Receivable			
		Interest Receivable			
		Interest Revenue			

Name ____________________

Section ____________ Date __________

3. a.

b.

c.

d.

e.

f.

6. A. 1. a. 1000 × .10 = 100.00 $6\overline{)100.00}$ = \$16.66   \$1016.66

b. 1,100 × .10 = 110.00 $4\overline{)110.00}$ = \$27.50   1,127.50

c. 1,000 × .09 = 90.00 $6\overline{)90.00}$ = \$15.00   1015.00

d. 1,000 × .12 = 120.00 $6\overline{)120.00}$ = \$20.00   1020.00

e. 1,000 × .12 = 120.00 $3\overline{)120.00}$ = \$40.00   1040.00

f. 6979 × .10 = 697.90 $6\overline{)697.90}$ = \$116.31   7095.31

g. 5,000 × .08 = 400.00 $4\overline{)400.00}$ = \$100.00   \$5100.00

Name ______________________ **PROBLEM 6.A.7. & ALTERNATE**

Section ____________ Date ____________

1) **General Journal** *PAGE*

Date		Account Names and Explanations	A/C #	Debit	Credit
		a)			
		b)			

2) General Journal *PAGE*

Date		Account Names and Explanations	A/C #	Debit	Credit
		a)			
		b)			

Name ____________________

Section ____________ Date ____________

PROBLEM 6.A.8. & ALTERNATE

General Journal

PAGE

Date		Account Names and Explanations	A/C #	Debit	Credit
		ADJUSTING ENTRIES			
		a.			
		b.			
		c.			

6A9 5,000
.12
10000
5000
600.00

150
4)600.00
4
20

50
3)150

Name ______________________ PROBLEM 6.A.9. & ALTERNATE

Section ____________ Date ____________

1) General Journal PAGE

Date		Account Names and Explanations	A/C #	Debit	Credit
19X4					
Nov	1	Notes Receivable		5000 —	
		Accounts Receivable – J+K Stores			5000 —
		Received 12%, 90 day note			
Dec	31	Interest Receivable		100 —	
		Interest Revenue (INCOME)			100 —
		To accrued interest J+K Stores			
19X5					
Jan	30	Cash		5150 —	
		Notes Receivable			5000 —
		accrued Interest Receivable			100 —
		Interest Revenue			50 —
		J+K Stores note collected			
19X4					
Nov	1	Accounts Payable – Marco		5000 —	
		Notes Payable			5000 —
		Incurred 12%, 90 days settlement A/P			
Dec	31	Interest Expense		100 —	
		Accrued Interest Payable			100 —
		To accrued interest on Marco note			
19X5					
Jan	30	Notes Payable		5000 —	
		Interest Payable		100 —	
		Interest Expense		50 —	
		Cash			5150 —
		Marco note paid			

2) **General Journal** *PAGE*

Date		Account Names and Explanations	A/C #	Debit	Credit

Name ______________________ PROBLEM 6.A.10.

Section ____________ Date __________

General Journal PAGE

Date		Account Names and Explanations	A/C #	Debit	Credit
19X4		1)			
Dec	31	Interest Receivable		40 —	
		Interest Revenue			40 —
		To accrued interest Horatio Alge			
19X5		2)			
Dec	31	Cash		2160 —	
		Interest Receivable			40 —
		Interest Revenue			120 —
		Notes Receivable			2000 —
		Paid Horatio Alge			

Name ______________________

Section ______________ Date ______________

PROBLEM 6.A.11.

General Journal

PAGE

Date		Account Names and Explanations	A/C #	Debit	Credit
19XX					
July	1	Accounts Receivable - Able		3000 —	
		Sales			3000 —
	3	Notes Receivable		4000 —	
		Accounts Receivable - Baker Co.			4000 —
		9% /60 days / overdue account			
	12	Cash		2030 —	
		Interest Revenue			30 —
		Notes Receivable			2000 —
		Paid - Charlie Company			
	22	Cash		4060 —	
		~~Interest Receivable~~			~~60~~
		Notes Receivable			4060 —
		Paid - Delta dishonored note			
	31	Notes Receivable		3000 —	
		Accounts Receivable - Able			3000 —
		9%, /60 day / balance due			

General Journal *PAGE*

Date		Account Names and Explanations	A/C #	Debit	Credit

Name ______________________

Section ____________ Date ____________

6B1

General Journal

PAGE

Date		Account Names and Explanations	A/C #	Debit	Credit
19xx		1. a.			
May	21	Uncollectible Accounts Exp		1200 —	
		Accounts Receivable—A.L. Windall			1200 —
May	21	b. Accounts Receivable—A.L. Windall		1200 —	
		Uncollectible Accounts Exp.			1200 —
		Cash		1200 —	
		Accounts Receivable			1200 —

6.B2.

General Journal PAGE

Date		Account Names and Explanations	A/C #	Debit	Credit
Dec	31	2. a. Uncollectible Allowance Expense 15%		11500 —	
		Allowance for doubtful Accounts			11500 —
		b.			

Name ____________________ **SELF-QUIZ FOR SECTION 6.B** *(Continued)*

Section ____________ Date ____________

6.B.3.

General Journal *PAGE*

Date		Account Names and Explanations	A/C #	Debit	Credit
Dec	31	3. a. Uncollectible Allowance Expence 4%		4300 —	
		Allowance for doubtful accounts			4300 —
6B4					
April	15	a. Allowance for doubtful accounts		2400 —	
		Accounts Receivable - Barry Co			2400 —
July	20	b. Accounts Receivable - Barry Co.		2400 —	
		Allowance for doubtful accounts			2400 —
		Cash		2400 —	
		Accounts Receivable - Barry Co			2400 —

General Journal *PAGE*

Date		Account Names and Explanations	A/C #	Debit	Credit
		4.			

5.

Name ______________________ **PROBLEM 6.B.6. & ALTERNATE**

Section ______________ Date ____________

General Journal *PAGE*

Date		Account Names and Explanations	A/C #	Debit	Credit
19--		1) Uncollectible Accounts Expence			
Dec	31	Allowance for doubtful accounts		2830 —	
					2830 —
		2)			
Dec	31	Uncollectible Accounts Expense		3530 —	
		Allowance for doubtful accounts			3530 —

6.B.1. 19xx

July 9 5 Uncollectible accounts 800
Accounts Receivable 800
Talleyhoe uncollectible account

6.B.1.b.

Nov. 10 Accounts Receivable 800
Uncollectible accounts 800
To reinstate written off account

10 Cash 800
Accounts Receivable - Talleyhoe 800
Payment of account

6.B.2.a.

19XX

March 12 Allowance for Doubtful Accounts 700
Accounts Receivable - Nile Company 700

Sept 14 Accounts Receivable - Nile Co. 700
Allowance for Doubtful Accounts 700

14 Cash 700
Accounts Receivable - Nile Co 700

6.B.3. a. Dec 31 Uncollectible Allowance Expense 1% 6000
Allowance for doubtful accounts 6000

b. Dec 31 Uncollectible Allowance Expense 5% 4,300
Allowance for doubtful accounts 4,300

6.B.4. Dec 31 Estimated Uncollectible 3,279
Allowance for doubtful accounts 3,279

Name ______________________

Section ____________ Date ____________

PROBLEM 6.B.7. & ALTERNATE

General Journal

PAGE

Date		Account Names and Explanations	A/C #	Debit	Credit
		1)			
		2)			

Name ______________________

Section ____________ Date ____________

PROBLEM 6.B.8. & ALTERNATE

General Journal

PAGE

Date		Account Names and Explanations	A/C #	Debit	Credit
		1)			
		2)			

Name ______________________

Section ____________ Date __________

PROBLEM 6.B.9.

EXAAM COMPANY
Partial Balance Sheet
December 31, 19--

Name ______________________ **PROBLEM 6.B.10.**

Section ______________ Date __________

BURNS COMPANY
Aging Schedule
July 1, 19--

Account	0-30 Days	31-60 Days	61-90 Days	Over 90 Days

Name ____________________ **PROBLEM 6.B.11.**

Section ____________ Date ____________

1)

2)

3) **General Journal** *PAGE*

Date	Account Names and Explanations	A/C #	Debit	Credit

Name ____________________

Section __________ Date __________

General Journal

PAGE

Date		Account Names and Explanations	A/C #	Debit	Credit

General Journal *PAGE*

Date		Account Names and Explanations	A/C #	Debit	Credit

Name ______________________ **PROBLEM 6.2. & ALTERNATE**

Section ____________ Date __________

1) A partially completed, ten-column work sheet for this requirement can be found at the back of this volume.

2)

R. H. MAYS COMPANY
Income Statement
For the Year Ended December 31, 19X4

3)

R. H. MAYS COMPANY
Balance Sheet
December 31, 19X4

Name ______________________ **PROBLEM 6.3. & ALTERNATE**

Section ______________ Date __________

1)

____

Receivables Aging Schedule

____

Customer	1-30 Days	31-60 Days	61-120 Days	Over 120 Days

General Journal *PAGE*

Date		Account Names and Explanations	A/C #	Debit	Credit
		2)			
		3)			

4) For Alternate Problem 6.3. only

Name ______________________ **COMPREHENSION PROBLEM 6.4.**

Section ____________ Date ____________

1)

2) **General Journal** *PAGE*

Date		Account Names and Explanations	A/C #	Debit	Credit

3)

Name

Section Date

COMPREHENSION PROBLEM 6.5.

1)

2)

Name ______________________________

Section ______________ Date ____________

1.

2. a.

b.

c.

3.

Name ______________________ PROBLEM 7.A.4. & ALTERNATE

Section ______________ Date ____________

$16,150

1) ~~LIFO~~ FIFO

100 units @ 20 = $2,000 $16,150
50 units @ 19 = 950 - 3,310
20 units @ 18 = 360 $12,840
$3,310

2) ~~FIFO~~ LIFO

80 units @ $15 = $1200 $16,150
90 units @ 16 = 1440 2640
$2640 $13510

3) *Weighted Average*

17.365) 93 16,15.000 ... 55

1737 X170 = 295290 Ending inv

$16,150
2953
$13,197

Name ______________________________

Section ________________ Date ____________

PROBLEM 7.A.5. & ALTERNATE

Cost of goods avail. for sale $13,200

1) a) ~~FIFO~~ LIFO

100 units @ $30 = $3000 — $13200

3000

Cost of goods sold — $10200

b) ~~LIFO~~ FIFO

100 units @ $36 = $3600 — $13,200

3600

Cost of goods sold — $9600

c) *Weighted Average*

400) 13200. = 33

1200

1200

1200

33 × 100 = 3300

$ 13,200

3300

$9900 cost of goods sold

12000

2) a) ***FIFO***

100 units @ 30 = 3000 $12000
3000
$9000

b) ***LIFO***

100 units @ 30 = $3000 $12000
3000
$9000

c) ***Weighted Average***

3000
400 ⟌ 12000

12,000
3000
9,000

Name ______________________ **PROBLEM 7.A.6. & ALTERNATE**

Section ____________ Date __________

1)

2)

Name ____________________

Section ____________ Date ____________

1.

2.

5700

3. a. ***FIFO***

Cost of goods sold

Sale of Jan 10	3 @ $500	1500
Sale of Jan 20	2 @ 500	1000
	2 @ 520	1040
	1 @ 540	540
Cost of goods sold		4080

Ending inventory
From purchase of Jan 15 3 @ 540 $1620

b. ***LIFO***

Cost of goods sold

Sale of Jan 20	4 @ 540	$2160
	1 @ 520	520
Sale of Jan 10	1 @ 520	520
	2 @ 500	1000
Cost of goods sold		$4200

Ending inventory
From purchase of Jan 1 3 @ 500 $1500

c. ***Moving Average***

Beginning inventory	5 @ 500	$2500 —	
Purchase Jan 5	2 @ 520	1040 —	
Available	7 @ 505.71	$3540 —	
Sold Jan. 10	3 @ 505.71	1517 13	$1517 13
Available	4 @ 505.71	2022 87	
Purchased Jan 15	4 @ 540.	2160 —	
Available	8 @ 522.86	$4182 87	
Sold Jan. 20	5 @ 522.86	2614 30	$2614 30
Inventory Jan. 31	3 @ 522.86	$1568 57	
Cost of goods sold			$4131 43

Name ________________________

Section ____________ Date __________

4.

5.

6.

Inventory Item	Quantity	Invoice Cost	Replacement Cost	Lower of Cost or Market
A	10	$ 50	$ 60	$______
B	30	10	8	______
C	5	80	85	______
D	22	32	30	______
E	4	100	100	______
F	15	16	20	______
Total Ending Inventory				$______

7.B.1. a. 11 12-2=10+3=13-2=11 $4450 4800

b. 11 12+3=15 2+2=4 pur. sold 15-4=11 $4400

7.B.2. $3000 11 6 units

4200

7500

1140

1750

$17,590 Total ending inventory

Name ______________________ PROBLEM 7.B.4. & ALTERNATE

Section ____________ Date ____________

1) a) *LIFO Periodic*

b) *FIFO Periodic*

c) *Weighted Average*

2) a) *LIFO Perpetual*

b) *FIFO Perpetual*

Name ______________________

Section ____________ Date __________

c) *Moving Average*

600
330
840
1770

60
+30
90
-40
50
+70
120
-80
40

Name ______________________________

Section ________________ Date ____________

1) *FIFO Perpetual*

Cost of goods sold

Sale of March 18	40 @ $10	$400
Sale of March 31	20 @ 10	200
	30 @ 11	330
	30 @ 12	360
Cost of goods sold		$1290

Ending inventory

From purchase of 3/27 | 40 @ 12 $480

2) *LIFO Perpetual*

Cost of goods sold

Sale of March 31	70 @ 12	$840
	10 @ 10	100
Sale of March 18	30 @ 11	330
	10 @ 10	100
Cost of goods sold		1370

Ending inventory

From March 1 | 40 @ 10 = $400

3) *Moving Average*

Beginning inventory	60	@	$10	$ 600 —
Purchase March 3	30	@	11	330 —
Available	90	@	10.33	930 —
Sold March 18	40	@	10.33	413 20
Available	50	@	10.33	516 80
Purchase March 27	70	@	12	840 —
Available	120	@	11.31	1356 80
Sold March 31	80	@	11.31	904 80
Inventory March 31 after sale	40	@	11.31	452 00

Cost of goods sold 413.20 + 904.80 = $1318

Name ______________________

Section ____________ Date ____________

PROBLEM 7.B.6. & ALTERNATE

Item: ____________________ **Location:** ____________________

Date	Received			Sold			Balance		
	Units	*Unit Cost*	*Amount*	*Units*	*Unit Cost*	*Amount*	*Units*	*Unit Cost*	*Amount*

Name ______________________ **PROBLEM 7.B.7.**

Section ____________ Date ____________

1) **General Journal** *PAGE*

Date		Account Names and Explanations	A/C #	Debit	Credit

2)

Name ______________________

Section ____________ Date __________

1.

2.

3. a.

b.

Name ____________________

Section __________ Date __________

4. a.

	Cost	Retail

b.

7C5

7.C.1. a. 50% of cost
b. 33% of selling price

66%
70 3/4% should be
120,000 stolen
99,000 est cost
58,500

7C2 a. 20%
b. 25%
c. $7
d. 43%
e. $15
f. 20%
g. 150%?

7.C.4.

Beginning inventory		$100,000
Purchases 1/1 - 6/30		400,000
Available for sale		500,000
Sales 1/1 - 6/30	800,000	
Less est. gross profit (45% x 800,000) =	360,000	
Estimated cost of goods sold		440,000
Estimated inventory at June 30		$ 60,000

Name ______________________

Section ____________ Date ____________

PROBLEM 7.C.5. & ALTERNATE

400,000
.70
28,000 00.00

	Cost	Retail	
Beginning inventory	$ 64,000 —	$ 96,000 —	
Purchases through May 14	300,000 —	424,000 —	
Goods available	364,000 —	520,000 —	70%
Sales through May 14 400,000		400,000 —	
Inventory Retail 5/14		120,000 —	
Inventory Retail 5/15		130,000 —	
Inventory Cost May 14	84,000 —		
Inventory at cost 5/15 cost	21,000 —		
	63,000 —	90,000 —	

Name ______________________

Section ______________ Date ______________

80000
-50400
29600

80000
.63
240000
480000
50,400.00

PROBLEM 7.C.6. & ALTERNATE

409500
29600
379900

	Cost	Retail
Beginning	30000 —	50000 —
Purchases	379500 —	600000 —
Cost of goods available	409500 —	650000 — 63
Sales		
Cost of goods sold	379900 —	
Ending Inventory	29600 —	80000 —

Name ____________________

Section ____________ Date ____________

PROBLEM 7.C.7. & ALTERNATE

1) **Cost** **Retail**

2)

Name ______________________________ PROBLEM 7.C.8.

Section ____________ Date ____________

STIFLE STORES
Income Statement
For the Year Ended December 31, 19X4

Sales		$140,000
Cost of goods sold		
Inventory, January 1	$ 20,000	
Net purchases	100,000	
Goods available for sale	$120,000	
Inventory, December 31	________	
Cost of goods sold		________
Gross Profit		$________

Calculations:

Name ______________________________ **PROBLEM 7.C.9.**

Section ______________ Date __________

Calculations:

VINNY SALES COMPANY
Income Statement
For Three Months Ended April 30, 19X5

Name ______________________

Section ____________ Date ____________

1)

2)

3)

4)

Name ________________________________

Section ______________ Date __________

PROBLEM 7.2. & ALTERNATE

A partially completed, ten-column work sheet for this problem can be found at the back of this volume. Use this space for any calculations necessary to complete the work sheet.

Name ______

Section ______ Date ______

PROBLEM 7.3. & ALTERNATE

1)

2)

Name ______________________

Section ____________ Date ____________

Name ______________________

Section ____________ Date ____________

COMPREHENSION PROBLEM 7.5.

1)

General Journal

PAGE

Date		Account Names and Explanations	A/C #	Debit	Credit
		ADJUSTING ENTRIES			

2)

3)

Name ____________________

Section ____________ Date ____________

COMPREHENSION PROBLEM 7.6.

1)

	19X4	19X3	19X2
Sales			
Cost of goods sold			
Gross Profit			
Operating expenses			
Net Income			

Calculations:

2)

Name ______________________

Section ____________ Date ____________

SELF-QUIZ FOR SECTION 8.A

1.

General Journal

PAGE

Date		Account Names and Explanations	A/C #	Debit	Credit
19--					
Jan	4	Machinery		20140 —	
		Cash			20140 —
	5	Machinery		300 —	
		Cash			300 —
	6	Machinery		700 —	
		Cash			700 —
	8	Cash		800 —	
		Accumulated Depreciation		7000 —	
		Loss on Sale of Machinery		200 —	
		Machinery			8000 —
	10	Automotive Equipment		14000 —	
		Accumulated Depreciation		8000 —	
		Automotive Equipment			10000 —
		Cash			12000 —
	11	Building		60000 —	
		Cash			60000 —
	15	Accumulated Depreciation		4000 —	
		Cash			4000 —

May 15

8.A.1. Machinery 9,800
~~2. a.~~ Cash 9,800
Machinery 185
Cash 185
Machinery 240
Cash 240

8.A.2.

Plant Assets	COST	ACCUM. DEPR.	BOOK VALUE
Land	$175,000		
Buildings	700,000	$190,000	$510,000
Furniture + Equipment	160,000	80,000	80,000
Total plant assets	$1035000	$270000	$765,000

8.A.3. 8000 cost — 1200 depreciation per year — overhaul
~~b.~~ -7000 acum depr — 3) 3600
1000 old value — Accum Depreciation 3000
+3000 overhaul — Cash 3000
4000 new value
-400 salvage
3600 new value

8.A.4. Land $60,000 — Goodwill
Building 360,000
Furniture 40,000
Equipment 50,000
Inventory 90,000
Goodwill 130,000
Cash $750,000

Name ______________________

Section ____________ Date ____________

PROBLEM 8.A.5. & ALTERNATE

SUBSIDIARY PLANT LEDGER RECORD

Item Stamping Machine General Ledger Account Machinery + Equipment

Serial Number SM-1156 Location Building A

Estimated Life 5yrs Estimated Salvage $1,400 Depr. per year $280

Date	Explanation	Cost			Accumulated Depreciation			Book Value
		Debit	Credit	Balance	Debit	Credit	Balance	
19X3 July 1	Cost	11,300		11,300				11,300
3	Freight	600		11,900				11,900
Dec 31	Depreciation/19X3				990	990	990	10910

Name ____________________
Section ______________ Date ______________

General Journal PAGE

Date		Account Names and Explanations	A/C #	Debit	Credit
19--					
June	8	Automotive Equipment (New)		17000 —	
		Accumulated Depreciation (OLD)		9000 —	
		~~Gain on trade in of old truck~~			~~3000~~
		Automotive Equipment (OLD)			12000 —
		Cash			14000 —
	15	Cash		12000 —	
		Accumulated Depreciation		10800 —	
		Machinery			12000 —
		Gain			1800 —
	18	Accum Depr ~~Overhaul~~ of machinery		2000 —	
		Cash			2000 —
	25	Equipment (Air conditioning)		200000 —	
		Cash			200000 —

Name ______________________ **PROBLEM 8.A.7. & ALTERNATE**

Section ____________ Date ____________

General Journal *PAGE*

Date		Account Names and Explanations	A/C #	Debit	Credit
19-3					
April	15	Equipment		96000 —	
		Accounts Payable 2/30, n/60			96000 —
	15	Freight Charges		2400 —	
		Cash			2400 —
	15	Installation Costs		1800 —	
		Cash			1800 —
May	1	Accounts Payable		96000 —	
		Purchas Discount			1920 —
		Cash			94080 —
19-7					
1	2	Accum depr ~~Overhaul of machinery~~		21615 —	
		Cash			21615 —

General Journal PAGE 7

Date		Account Names and Explanations	A/C #	Debit	Credit
19--					
1	5	Cash		29000 —	
		Accumulated Depreciation		48000 —	
		Automotive Equipment (Bus)			80000 —
		Loss on Sale		3000 —	
				10000 —	
1	5	Cash		~~29000~~ —	
		Accumulated Depreciation		43000 —	
		Equipment			50000 —
		Gain			~~22000~~ —
					3000 —
1	5	Cash		400 —	
		Accumulated Depreciation		7600 —	
		Machinery			8000 —

Name ____________________ PROBLEM 8.A.9

Section __________ Date __________

General Journal *PAGE*

Date		Account Names and Explanations	A/C #	Debit	Credit
19x2					
1	2	Office furniture		10000 —	
		Accounts Payable			10000 —
	5	Installation + Delivery cost		200 —	
		Cash			200 —
	10	Accounts Payable		10000 —	
		Discount on purchase			200 —
		Cash			9800 —
12	31	Accumulated Depreciation		1800 —	
		Depreciation Expense			1800 —
19x3					
12	31	Accumulated Depreciation		1800 —	
		Depreciation Expense			1800 —
19x4		Accumulated Depr		1800 —	
12	31	Depr exp			1800 —
19x5					
7	1	Cash		4000 —	
		Accumulated Depreciation		4600 —	
		Loss on sale		1400 —	
		Office Furniture			10000 —

Name ____________________ **PROBLEM 8.A.9.**

Section ____________ Date ____________

1) **General Journal** *PAGE*

Date		Account Names and Explanations	A/C #	Debit	Credit

General Journal *PAGE*

Date		Account Names and Explanations	A/C #	Debit	Credit
		2)			

Name ______________________ **SELF-QUIZ FOR SECTION 8.B**

Section ____________ Date ____________

1. **General Journal** *PAGE*

Date		Account Names and Explanations	A/C #	Debit	Credit
		a.			
		b.			
		c.			
		d.			

2.

Method	Size of Reported Net Income	Size of Reported Total Assets
Straight-line		
Double-declining-balance		
Sum-of-years'-digits		

3. and 4. **General Journal** *PAGE*

Date		Account Names and Explanations	A/C #	Debit	Credit

Name ____________________

Section ____________ Date ____________

General Journal

PAGE

Date		Account Names and Explanations	A/C #	Debit	Credit
		1)			
		2)			
		3)			
		4)			

Name ______________________

Section ______________ Date ______________

Depreciation				
Date	*Straight-Line*	*Sum-of-Years'-Digits*	*Double-Declining-Balance*	*150% Declining Balance*
12/31/X3				
12/31/X4				
12/31/X5				
12/31/X6				
12/31/X7				
Total				

Name ____________________ PROBLEM 8.B.10. & ALTERNATE

Section ____________ Date ____________

1), 2) and 3) **General Journal** *PAGE*

Date		Account Names and Explanations	A/C #	Debit	Credit

Name ______________________ **PROBLEM 8.B.11.**

Section ______________ Date ______________

General Journal *PAGE*

Date		Account Names and Explanations	A/C #	Debit	Credit
		a.			
		b.			
		c.			
		d.			

Name ____________________ **PROBLEM 8.B.12.**

Section __________ Date __________

General Journal *PAGE*

Date		Account Names and Explanations	A/C #	Debit	Credit
		1)			
		2)			

Name ______________________________

Section ______________ Date ____________

PROBLEM 8.B.13.

1)

2)

Name ______________________________

Section ______________ Date ____________

PROBLEM 8.1. & ALTERNATE

General Journal *PAGE*

Date		Account Names and Explanations	A/C #	Debit	Credit
		1)			
		2) a)			
		b)			

General Journal *PAGE*

Date		Account Names and Explanations	A/C #	Debit	Credit
		c)			

Name ______________________________

Section ______________ Date ______________

PROBLEM 8.2. & ALTERNATE

General Journal

PAGE

Date		Account Names and Explanations	A/C #	Debit	Credit
		1)			
		2)			
		3)			

General Journal

PAGE

Date		Account Names and Explanations	A/C #	Debit	Credit
		4)			
		5)			

Name ______________________

Section ______________ Date ____________

PROBLEM 8.3. & ALTERNATE

1) A partially completed, ten-column work sheet for this requirement can be found at the back of this volume.

2)

____

Income Statement

____

3)

Balance Sheet

Name ____________________

Section ____________ Date ____________

PROBLEM 8.4. & ALTERNATE

1) and 3) **General Journal** *PAGE*

Date		Account Names and Explanations	A/C #	Debit	Credit

2) and 4)

SUBSIDIARY PLANT LEDGER RECORD

Item ______________________ General Ledger Account ______________________

Serial Number ______________________ Location ______________________

Estimated Life ____________ Estimated Salvage ____________ Depr. per year ______________________

Date	Explanation	Cost			Accumulated Depreciation			Book Value
		Debit	*Credit*	*Balance*	*Debit*	*Credit*	*Balance*	

Name ______________________________

Section ______________ Date ______________

PROBLEM 8.5.

General Journal

PAGE

Date		Account Names and Explanations	A/C #	Debit	Credit
		1)			
		2)			
		3)			
		4)			

Name ______________________

Section ____________ Date ____________

COMPREHENSION PROBLEM 8.6.

1)

2)

General Journal *PAGE*

Date		Account Names and Explanations	A/C #	Debit	Credit
		a)			

General Journal *PAGE*

Date		Account Names and Explanations	A/C #	Debit	Credit
		b)			
		c)			
		d)			

Name ______________________

Section ____________ Date ____________

3)

Name ____________________ **COMPREHENSION PROBLEM 8.7.**

Section __________ Date __________

1)	
2)	

3)

4)

Name ______________________

Section ____________ Date ____________

1.

2.

3. **General Journal** *PAGE*

Date		Account Names and Explanations	A/C #	Debit	Credit

4.

Name ______________________ **PROBLEM 9.A.7. & ALTERNATE**

Section ______________ Date __________

1)

PETTY CASH VOUCHER

No. ________

Amount $ ____________ **Date** ____________

Paid to ______________________________

For ______________________________

Charge to ______________________________

Approved by ______________________________

Received by ______________________________

9.A.2.

19--			
June 1	Petty Cash Fund	150	
	Cash		150
30	Travel Expense	49	
	Postage Expense	18	
	Entertainment Expense	27	
	Cash		94

2) **General Journal** *PAGE*

Date		Account Names and Explanations	A/C #	Debit	Credit

Name ______________________

Section ____________ Date ____________

General Journal PAGE

Date		Account Names and Explanations	A/C #	Debit	Credit
19--					
Feb	3	Petty Cash Fund		100 —	
		Cash			100 —
	16	Postage Expense		13 —	
		Travel Expense		74 —	
		Freight Expense		8 —	
		Cash Short + Over		1 —	
		Cash			96 —

Name ______________________ **PROBLEM 9.A.9. & ALTERNATE**

Section __________ Date __________

1)

PETTY CASH VOUCHER

No. ________

Amount $ ________ **Date** ________

Paid to ______________________

For ______________________

Charge to ______________________

Approved by ______________________

Received by ______________________

2) General Journal *PAGE*

Date		Account Names and Explanations	A/C #	Debit	Credit

Name ____________________

Section __________ Date __________

PROBLEM 9.A.10.

General Journal *PAGE*

Date		Account Names and Explanations	A/C #	Debit	Credit

Name ______________________

Section ____________ Date ____________

SELF-QUIZ FOR SECTION 9.B

1.

2.

3. 1)

DUNKLE COMPANY
Bank Reconciliation
May 31, 19--

BANK STATEMENT			*BOOKS*		

Name ____________________

Section ______________ Date ____________

2)

General Journal

PAGE

Date		Account Names and Explanations	A/C #	Debit	Credit

Name

Section Date

PROBLEM 9.B.6. & ALTERNATE

1)

Josh Redram Co

Bank Reconciliation

June 30, 19--

BANK STATEMENT			BOOKS		
Statement Balance		5755 61	Account Balance		5755 61
Add Deposit in transit	1673 50	1673 50	Add. Mistake in check amount		9 00
		7429 11			5764 61
Less Outstanding Checks	2142 —	2142 —	Less Returned Check	189 —	
			Unrecorded Check	274 50	
			Service Charge	14 —	477 50
Disposable Cash		5287 11	Disposable Cash		5287 11

2) General Journal *PAGE*

Date		Account Names and Explanations	A/C #	Debit	Credit
19--					
June	30	Cash in Bank		9 —	
		Accounts Payable			9 —
		Error in recording check			
		Accounts Receivable		189 —	
		Cash in Bank			189 —
		Returned Check			
		Accounts Payable		274 50	
		Cash in Bank			274 50
		Bank Service Charge		14 —	
		Cash in Bank			14 —

Name ______________________

Section ____________ Date ________

PROBLEM 9.B.7. & ALTERNATE

1)

Bank Reconciliation

BANK STATEMENT			*BOOKS*		

2) General Journal *PAGE*

Date		Account Names and Explanations	A/C #	Debit	Credit

Name ______________________

Section ____________ Date ________

PROBLEM 9.B.8. & ALTERNATE

1)

Bank Reconciliation

BANK STATEMENT			BOOKS		

2) **General Journal** *PAGE*

Date		Account Names and Explanations	A/C #	Debit	Credit

3)

Name ______________________ PROBLEM 9.B.9.

Section ____________ Date ________

1)

FERNANDEZ COMPANY
Bank Reconciliation
May 31, 19--

BANK STATEMENT			*BOOKS*		

2) **General Journal** *PAGE*

Date		Account Names and Explanations	A/C #	Debit	Credit

Name ______________________

Section ____________ Date ________

PROBLEM 9.1. & ALTERNATE

Bank Reconciliation

BANK STATEMENT			CHECKBOOK		

Name ____________________

Section ____________ Date ________

1)

____

Bank Reconciliation

____

____

BANK STATEMENT			BOOKS		

2) **General Journal** *PAGE*

Date		Account Names and Explanations	A/C #	Debit	Credit

3)

4)

Name ____________________

Section ____________ Date ________

PROBLEM 9.3. & ALTERNATE

1)

Bank Reconciliation

BANK STATEMENT			BOOKS		

2)

Name ______________________

Section ____________ Date ________

PROBLEM 9.4.

1)

NAOMI SALES COMPANY
Bank Reconciliation
March 31, 19--

BANK STATEMENT			*BOOKS*		

2) **General Journal** *PAGE*

Date		Account Names and Explanations	A/C #	Debit	Credit

3)

Name ______________________________

Section ______________ Date ____________

COMPREHENSION PROBLEM 9.5.

1)

Calculation of amount embezzled:

2)

Name ______________________

Section ____________ Date __________

COMPREHENSION PROBLEM 9.6.

Name ______________________________

Section ______________ Date __________

1.

2.

3. a.

VOUCHER No. ______________

Pay to ______________________________ Voucher Date ______________________________
______________________________ Invoice Date ______________________________
______________________________ Due Date ______________________________

Invoice No. ______________________________ Gross Amount $______________
P.O. No. ______________________________ Discount ______________
Net $______________

Verifications

Quantities	______________
Prices	______________
Terms	______________
Extensions and Footings	______________
Account Distribution	______________
Approved	______________

Account Distribution

Account	*Amount*
______________	$ ______________
______________	______________
______________	______________
______________	______________
Vouchers Payable (Cr.)	$ ______________

Paid: ______________________________ Check No. ______________ Amount $ ______________

b. A voucher register for this requirement can be found at the back of this volume.

Name ____________________

Section ____________ Date __________

c.

CHECK REGISTER

PAGE

Check No.	Date	Payee	Voucher No.	Vouchers Payable Dr.	Purchases Discounts Cr.	Cash Cr.

4.

Name ______________________________ **PROBLEM 10.A.4. & ALTERNATE**

Section ______________ Date __________

1)

VOUCHER No. __________

Pay to ______________________ **Voucher Date** ______________________

______________________ **Invoice Date** ______________________

______________________ **Due Date** ______________________

Invoice No. ______________________ **Gross Amount** $______________

P.O. No. ______________________ **Discount** ______________

Net $______________

Verifications

Quantities	
Prices	
Terms	
Extensions and Footings	
Account Distribution	
Approved	

Account Distribution

Account	*Amount*
	$
Vouchers Payable (Cr.)	$

Paid: ______________________ **Check No.** ______________ **Amount** $ ______________

2) and 3) A voucher register for these requirements can be found at the back of this volume.

Name ____________ **PROBLEM 10.A.5. & ALTERNATE**

Section ________ Date ________

1)

VOUCHER **No.** 101

Pay to ____________ **Voucher Date** ____________

____________ **Invoice Date** ____________

____________ **Due Date** ____________

Invoice No. ____________ **Gross Amount** $____________

P.O. No. ____________ **Discount** ____________

Net $____________

Verifications

Quantities ____________

Prices ____________

Terms ____________

Extensions and Footings ____________

Account Distribution ____________

Approved ____________

Account Distribution	
Account	***Amount***
	$
Vouchers Payable (Cr.)	$

Paid: ____________ **Check No.** ____________ **Amount** $____________

VOUCHER No. 102

Pay to ____________________ Voucher Date ____________________
____________________ Invoice Date ____________________
____________________ Due Date ____________________

Invoice No. ____________________ Gross Amount $ ____________________
P.O. No. ____________________ Discount ____________________
Net $ ____________________

Verifications

Quantities ____________________
Prices ____________________
Terms ____________________
Extensions and Footings ____________________
Account Distribution ____________________
Approved ____________________

Account Distribution	
Account	*Amount*
	$
Vouchers Payable (Cr.)	$

Paid: ____________________ Check No. ____________________ Amount $ ____________________

VOUCHER No. 103

Pay to		Voucher Date	
		Invoice Date	
		Due Date	
Invoice No.		Gross Amount	$
P.O. No.		Discount	
		Net	$

Verifications

Quantities	
Prices	
Terms	
Extensions and Footings	
Account Distribution	
Approved	

Account Distribution

Account	*Amount*
	$
Vouchers Payable (Cr.)	$

Paid: ______________ Check No. __________ Amount $ __________

2) A voucher register for this requirement can be found at the back of this volume.

3) CHECK REGISTER *PAGE*

Check No.	Date	Payee	Voucher No.	Vouchers Payable Dr.	Purchases Discounts Cr.	Cash Cr.

Name ______________________ PROBLEM 10.A.6. & ALTERNATE

Section ____________ Date ____________

VOUCHER No. ____________

Pay to ______________________ Voucher Date ______________________

______________________ Invoice Date ______________________

______________________ Due Date ______________________

Invoice No. ______________________ Gross Amount $______________

P.O. No. ______________________ Discount ______________

Net $______________

Verifications

Quantities ______________

Prices ______________

Terms ______________

Extensions and Footings ______________

Account Distribution ______________

Approved ______________

Account Distribution	
Account	*Amount*
______________	$ ________
______________	________
______________	________
______________	________
Vouchers Payable (Cr.)	$ ________

Paid: ______________________ Check No. ____________ Amount $ ____________

Name ____________________

Section __________ Date __________

PROBLEM 10.A.8.

CHECK REGISTER

PAGE

Check No.	Date	Payee	Voucher No.	Vouchers Payable Dr.	Purchases Discounts Cr.	Cash Cr.

Name ______________________

Section ______________ Date __________

SELF-QUIZ FOR SECTION 10.B

1.

2. a.

b.

3. **General Journal** *PAGE*

Date		Account Names and Explanations	A/C #	Debit	Credit
		a.			
		b.			

Name ____________________

Section __________ Date __________

PROBLEM 10.B.7. & ALTERNATE

General Journal

PAGE

Date		Account Names and Explanations	A/C #	Debit	Credit
		1)			
		2)			
		3)			

Name ____________________

Section ____________ Date ____________

PROBLEM 10.B.8. & ALTERNATE

General Journal

PAGE

Date		Account Names and Explanations	A/C #	Debit	Credit
		1)			
		2)			
		3)			
		4)			

Name ______________________

Section ____________ Date ____________

PROBLEM 10.B.9. & ALTERNATE

YEAR ____

EMPLOYEE'S INDIVIDUAL EARNINGS RECORD

NAME ______________________ Social Security No. ______________________

ADDRESS ______________________ Birthdate ______________________

______________________ Employment Date ______________________

Phone ______________________ Termination Date ______________________

Classification ______________________ Tax Status: ☐ Married ☐ Single

Pay Rate ______________________ No. Allowances ______________________

Period Ending	Earnings				Deductions				Net Pay
	Regular	*Premium*	*Gross*	*Cumulative*	*Federal Income Tax*	*FICA Tax*	*Union Dues*	*Total*	

Name ____________________ **PROBLEM 10.1. & ALTERNATE**

Section __________ Date __________

A voucher register required for this problem can be found at the back of this volume.

CHECK REGISTER *PAGE*

Check No.	Date		Payee	Voucher No.	Vouchers Payable Dr.	Purchases Discounts Cr.	Cash Cr.

Name ____________________

Section ____________ Date ____________

1) and 3) A partially completed voucher register for these requirements can be found at the back of this volume.

CHECK REGISTER

PAGE 38

Check No.	Date	Payee	Voucher No.	Vouchers Payable Dr.	Purchases Discounts Cr.	Cash Cr.
		Brought Forward		125,60048	92 61	124,67 87

2)

ACCOUNT NO.

Date		Item	Ref.	Debit	Credit	Balance	
						Debit	*Credit*

ACCOUNT NO.

Date		Item	Ref.	Debit	Credit	Balance	
						Debit	*Credit*

ACCOUNT NO.

Date		Item	Ref.	Debit	Credit	Balance	
						Debit	*Credit*

Name ______________________

Section ____________ Date __________

PROBLEM 10.3. & ALTERNATE

1)

		Earnings Subject to		
Employee	*FICA*	*Unemployment*	*Retirement*	Withholding

Computation of employees' withholding:

2) Computation of employer's payroll tax and retirement contributions:

3) General Journal *PAGE*

Date		Account Names and Explanations	A/C #	Debit	Credit

Name ____________

Section ________ Date ________

PROBLEM 10.4. & ALTERNATE

1)

PAYROLL REGISTER

For biweekly period ending ____________

Name	Hours	Regular Rate	Earnings			Deductions				Net Pay
			Regular	*Overtime Premium*	*Gross*	*Federal Income Tax*	*FICA Tax*	*Union Dues*	*Total*	

2)

YEAR ____

EMPLOYEE'S INDIVIDUAL EARNINGS RECORD

NAME ____ Social Security No. ____

ADDRESS ____ Birthdate ____

____ Employment Date ____

Phone ____ Termination Date ____

Classification ____ Tax Status: ☐ Married ☐ Single

Pay Rate ____ No. Allowances ____

Period Ending	Earnings				Deductions				Net Pay
	Regular	*Premium*	*Gross*	*Cumulative*	*Federal Income Tax*	*FICA Tax*	*Union Dues*	*Total*	

Name ____________________

Section ____________ Date ____________

3) **General Journal** *PAGE*

Date		Account Names and Explanations	A/C #	Debit	Credit

Name ______________________________

Section ______________ Date __________

COMPREHENSION PROBLEM 10.5.

Name ______________________________

Section ______________ Date __________

1.

2.

3.

4.

5. a.

b.

c.

d.

e.

f.

Name ______________________________

Section ______________ Date ____________

Chart of Accounts

Account Number	*Account*

Name ________________________________

Section ______________ Date ____________

PROBLEM 11.5. & ALTERNATE

1	2	3	4	5	6	7	8	9	10	11	12	13	14	15	16	17	18	19	20	21	22	23

Name ______________________ **PROBLEM 11.6.**

Section ______________ Date ____________

1)

2)

Name ______________________

Section ____________ Date __________

Name ________________

Section ________ Date ________

COMPREHENSION PROBLEM 11.8.

Name ______________________

Section ____________ Date __________

1.

2.

3. a.

b.

c.

d.

e.

4.

Name ______________________

Section ____________ Date __________

PROBLEM 12.A.5. & ALTERNATE

1)

2)

	19X4 Net Income	December 31, 19X4 *Assets*	December 31, 19X4 *Owner's Equity*
As reported			

Name ______________________

Section ____________ Date ____________

PROBLEM 12.A.6. & ALTERNATE

1)

2)

General Journal *PAGE*

Date		Account Names and Explanations	A/C #	Debit	Credit

3)

Name

Section Date

PROBLEM 12.A.7.

1)

2)

3)

4)

Name

Section Date

1.

2. a. Assets:

b. Net incomes:

c. Rates of return:

d. Sales growth trends:

Name ______________________

Section ____________ Date ____________

3. a.

b.

	Nominal Dollars	
	12/31/X9	*12/31/X8*

	Nominal Dollars	Conversion Factor	Constant 12/31/X9 Dollars

Name ________________

Section ________ Date ________

4. a.

b.

c.

5.

Name ______________________

Section ____________ Date ____________

PROBLEM 12.B.7. & ALTERNATE

1)

2)

Name ____________________

Section __________ Date __________

PROBLEM 12.B.8. & ALTERNATE

1)

2)

3)

Name ______________________

Section ____________ Date ____________

PROBLEM 12.B.9. & ALTERNATE

Name ______________________________

Section ______________ Date ___________

PROBLEM 12.B.10.

	Nominal Dollars	
	12/31/X9	*12/31/X8*

	Nominal Dollars	Conversion Factor	Constant 12/31/X9 Dollars

Name ______________________

Section ____________ Date ____________

PROBLEM 12.B.11.

Name ______________________

Section ____________ Date ____________

PROBLEM 12.1. & ALTERNATE

1)

	Nominal Dollars 12/31/	Nominal Dollars 12/31/

	Nominal Dollars	Conversion Factor	Constant 12/31/ Dollars

2)

Comparative Balance Sheet

	12/31/	12/31/
ASSETS		
Cash		
Accounts receivable		
Inventory (LIFO basis)		
Building and equipment (net)		
Land		
Total Assets		
LIABILITIES		
Accounts payable		
Note payable		
Total Liabilities		
OWNER'S EQUITY		
, capital		
Total Liabilities and Owner's Equity		

Calculations:

Name ______________________ PROBLEM 12.1. & ALTERNATE *(Concluded)*

Section ____________ Date __________

3)

Name ________________

Section ________ Date ________

PROBLEM 12.2. & ALTERNATE

1)

Income Statement

	Nominal Dollars	Adjustment Factor	Constant 12/31/ Dollars
Sales			
Cost of goods sold			
Gross Profit			
Operating expenses			
Depreciation			
Other			
Total operating expenses			
Operating Income			
Net monetary gain (loss)			
Net Income			

2)

Name ______________________ **PROBLEM 12.3. & ALTERNATE**

Section ______________ Date ______________

1)

____

Balance Sheet

____

____

	Nominal Dollars	Adjustment Factor	Constant 12/31/ Dollars
ASSETS			
Cash			
Accounts receivable			
Inventory (LIFO basis)			
Building and equipment (net)			
Land			
Total Assets			
LIABILITIES			
Accounts payable			
Notes (or Mortgage) payable			
Total Liabilities			
OWNER'S EQUITY			
, capital			
Total Liabilities and Owner's Equity			

2)

3)

Name ____________________

Section __________ Date __________

PROBLEM 12.4.

1)

BRINKERTON COMPANY
Income Statement
For the Year Ended December 31, 19X9

	Nominal Dollars	Adjustment Factor	Constant 12/31/X9 Dollars

Calculation of purchasing power gain (loss) during 19X9:

2)

3)

4)

Name ____________________

Section ____________ Date ____________

PROBLEM 12.5.

1)

2)

Name ______________________

Section ____________ Date ____________

COMPREHENSION PROBLEM 12.6.

1)

General Journal

PAGE

Date		Account Names and Explanations	A/C #	Debit	Credit

2)

3)

4)

Name ______________________

Section ____________ Date __________

1)

2)

Name ______________________

Section ______________ Date __________

COMPREHENSION PROBLEM 12.8.

1)

2)

Name ______________________

Section ____________ Date __________

1.

DIBBS CO[M]

Work Sh[eet]

For the Month o[f]

A/C #	Account	Unadjusted Trial Balance Dr.	Unadjusted Trial Balance Cr.
111	Cash	450	
112	Accounts Receivable	520	
113	Supplies	190	
115	Land	5000	
116	Building	25000	
0116	Accumulated Depreciation–Building		4500
211	Accounts Payable		110
212	Wages Payable		-0-
215	Mortgage Payable		10000
311	B. Dibbs, Capital		15850
312	B. Dibbs, Withdrawals	850	
411	Service Revenue		3200
511	Wage Expense	1400	
512	Supplies Expense	250	
513	Depreciation Expense	-0-	
		33660	33660

PANY

eet

April, 19--

Adjustments		Adjusted Trial Balance		Income Statement		Balance Sheet	
r.	Cr.	Dr.	Cr.	Dr.	Cr.	Dr.	Cr.
	2000 –						
00 –							

Name ______________________

Section ______________ Date ____________

G. Davi...

Work Sh...

Decemb...

A/C #	Account	Unadjusted Trial Balance Dr.	Unadjusted Trial Balance Cr.
	Cash	3950 —	
	Accounts Receivable	4100 —	
	Office Equipment	3000 —	
	Supplies	330 —	
	Accounts Payable		600 —
	G. Davis, Capital		3000 —
	Fees Earned		13655 —
	Salary Expense	4000 —	
	Utilities Expense	875 —	
	Rent Expense	1000 —	
	Accum. Depreciation	17255 —	17255 —
	Depreciation expense		
	Supplies Expense		
	Net Income		

et

31, 19—

Adjustments		Adjusted Trial Balance		Income Statement		Balance Sheet	
Dr.	Cr.	Dr.	Cr.	Dr.	Cr.	Dr.	Cr.
		3950 —				3950 —	
		4100 —				4100 —	
		3000 —				3000 —	
	90 —	240 —				240 —	
	200 —		800 —				800 —
			3000 —				3000 —
			13655 —		13655 —		
		4000 —		4090 —			
		875 —		875 —			
0 —		1200 —		800 —			
	600 —		600 —				
0 —		600 —		600 —			600 —
10 —		18055 —	18055 —	90 —			
90 —	890 —			6765 —	13655		
				6890 —		11290 —	4400 —
				13655 —	13655 —		6890 —
						11290 —	11290 —

...any

...19—

Adjustments	Adjusted Trial Balance		Income Statement		Balance Sheet	
Cr.	Dr.	Cr.	Dr.	Cr.	Dr.	Cr.
	600 —				600 —	
	1150 —				1150 —	
70 —	20 —				20 —	
	6800 —				6800 —	
170 —		510 —				510 —
		800 —				800 —
40 —		40 —				40 —
		4000 —				4000 —
		2550 —				2550 —
	500 —				500 —	
150 —		2150 —		2150 —		
	700 —		700 —			
	40 —		40 —			
	70 —		70 —			
	170 —		170 —			
430 —	10050 —	10050 —				
			1070 —			1170 —
			2150 —	2150 —	9070 —	9070 —

Name ____________________

Section ______________ Date ______________

1)

Link C
Work
March

A/C #	Account	Unadjusted Trial Balance Dr.	Unadjusted Trial Balance Cr.
11	Cash	600 —	
12	Accounts Receivable	1000 —	
13	Supplies	90 —	
15	Truck	6800 —	
015	Accumulated Depreciation - Truck		340 —
21	Accounts Payable		800 —
22	Interest Payable		-0-
23	Note Payable		4000 —
31	F. Lunk, Capital		2550 —
32	F. Lunk, Withdrawal	500 —	
41	Fees Earned		2000 —
51	Rent Expense	700 —	
52	Interest Expense	-0-	
53	Supplies Expense	-0-	
54	Depreciation Expense	-0-	
		9690 —	9690 —
	Net Income		

EPAIR

ber 31, 19--

ustments	Adjusted Trial Balance		Income Statement		Balance Sheet	
Cr.	Dr.	Cr.	Dr.	Cr.	Dr.	Cr.
	3475				3475	
	3025				3025	
	5500				5500	
b) 2850	2550				2550	
	10100				10100	
	17500				17500	
e) 875		4375				4375
	5000				5000	
f) 500	2500				2500	
d) 100		4675				4675
		31925				31925
		15400		15400		
	4950		4950			
	3500				3500	
a) 450		450				
	2850		2850			
	100		100			
	875		875			
	500		500			

Name ______________________________

Section ______________ Date __________

1) and 3)

MARTINEZ A

Work

For the Year Ende

A/C #	Account	Unadjusted Trial Balance Dr.	Unadjusted Trial Balance Cr.	
	Cash	3475		
	Accounts Receivable	3025		
	Prepaid Rent	5200		c)
	Supplies	5400		
	Land	10100		
	Building	17500		
	Accumulated Depreciation–Building		3500	
	Equipment	5000		
	Accumulated Depreciation–Equipment		2000	
	Accounts Payable		4575	
	P. Martinez, Capital		31925	
	Service Fees		15400	
	Wage Expense	4500		a)
	Rent Expense	3200		c)
		57400	57400	
	Wages Payable			
	Supplies Expense			b) 2
	Repair Expense			d)
	Depreciation Expense–Building			e)
	Depreciation Expense–Equipment			f)

NY

il, 19--

djustments		Adjusted Trial Balance		Income Statement		Balance Sheet	
	Cr.	Dr.	Cr.	Dr.	Cr.	Dr.	Cr.

Name ______________________

Section ____________ Date __________

2)

MARCO C

Work

For the Month

A/C #	Account	Unadjusted Trial Balance Dr.	Cr.
11	Cash	500	
12	Accounts Receivable	2000	
13	Supplies	900	
14	Prepaid Insurance	800	
16	Equipment	6000	
016	Accumulated Depreciation–Equipment		800
21	Accounts Payable		1800
22	Notes Payable		1500
23	Wages Payable		-0-
24	Interest Payable		-0-
31	E. Marco, Capital		4000
41	E. Marco, Withdrawals	900	
51	Service Revenue		8000
61	Wage Expense	4000	
62	Rent Expense	1000	
63	Supplies Expense	-0-	
64	Interest Expense	-0-	
65	Depreciation Expense	-0-	
66	Insurance Expense	-0-	
		16100	16100

Explanations

a) Supplies used during April, $400.

b) Insurance expired during April, $100.

c) Equipment depreciation for April, $200.

d) Accrued wages at April 30, $150.

e) Accrued interest at April 30, $20.

...ustments		Adjusted Trial Balance		Income Statement		Balance Sheet	
	Cr.	Dr.	Cr.	Dr.	Cr.	Dr.	Cr.

Name ____________________

Section ____________ Date ____________

4)

Work

A/C #	Account	Unadjusted Trial Balance	
		Dr.	Cr.

Name ______________________________

Section ______________ Date ____________

1)

ACE F

For the M

A/C #	Account	Unadjusted Trial Balance Dr.	Unadjusted Trial Balance Cr.
111	Cash	2000	
112	Accounts Receivable	4400	
113	Supplies	500	
116	Planes	250000	
116	Accumulated Depreciation—Planes		25000
211	Accounts Payable		5000
212	Interest Payable		-0-
213	Notes Payable (60 days)		6000
214	Loans Payable (due in 5 years)		100000
311	Fred Ace, Capital		118100
312	Fred Ace, Withdrawals	4000	
411	Charter Fees		15450
511	Salary Expense	6000	
512	Gasoline Expense	1650	
513	Rent Expense	1000	
514	Interest Expense	-0-	
515	Supplies Expense	-0-	
516	Depreciation Expense	-0-	
		269550	269550
	Explanations		
	a) Fees earned but not billed in January.		
	b) Supplies used in January.		
	c) Plane depreciation for January.		
	d) Interest accrued at January 31.		

PROBLEM 3.2. *(ALTERNATE ON REVERSE SIDE)*

PANY

eet

April, 19--

Adjustments		Adjusted Trial Balance		Income Statement		Balance Sheet	
	Cr.	*Dr.*	*Cr.*	*Dr.*	*Cr.*	*Dr.*	*Cr.*
		1000					
		6800					
	c) 300	1800					
	a) 200	2200					
	b) 750	8250					
		16400					
	d) 150		1750				
			7700				
	e) 450		450				
			10000				
			8000				
			8000				
		1000					
			13000				
0		9850					
0		200					
0		750					
0		300					
		200					
0		150					
0	1850	48900	48900				

Name ____________________

Section ____________ Date ____________

1)

T.D.S.

W

For the Mo

A/C #	Account	Unadjusted Trial Balance Dr.	Unadjusted Trial Balance Cr.	
11	Cash	1000		
12	Accounts Receivable	6800		
13	Supplies	2100		
14	Prepaid Insurance	2400		
15	Prepaid Rent	9000		
16	Equipment	16400		
016	Accumulated Depreciation–Equipment		1600	
21	Accounts Payable		7700	
22	Wages Payable		-0-	
23	Notes Payable (90 days)		10000	
24	Notes Payable (due in 7 years)		8000	
31	T.D. Sands, Capital		8000	
32	T.D. Sands, Withdrawals	1000		
41	Service Revenue		13000	
51	Wage Expense	9400		e)
52	Insurance Expense	-0-		a)
53	Rent Expense	-0-		b)
54	Supplies Expense	-0-		c)
55	Interest Expense	200		
56	Depreciation Expense	-0-		d)
		48300	48300	

Explanations

a) Insurance expired in April.

b) Prepaid rent expired in April.

c) Supplies used in April.

d) Equipment depreciation for April.

e) Accrued wages for April.

G SERVICE

heet

f January, 19--

Adjustments		Adjusted Trial Balance		Income Statement		Balance Sheet	
Dr.	Cr.	Dr.	Cr.	Dr.	Cr.	Dr.	Cr.
		20 00					
8 00		52 00					
	b) 4 70	30					
		2 500 00					
	c) 15 00		265 00				
			50 00				
	d) 9 50		9 50				
			60 00				
			1 000 00				
			1 181 00				
		40 00					
	a) 8 00		162 50				
		60 00					
		16 50					
		10 00					
9 50		9 50					
4 70		4 70					
5 00		15 00					
7 20	37 20	2 728 00	2 728 00				

stments		Adjusted Trial Balance		Income Statement		Balance Sheet	
	Cr.	*Dr.*	*Cr.*	*Dr.*	*Cr.*	*Dr.*	*Cr.*

Name ______________________________

Section ______________ Date __________

1)

____

Work

A/C #	Account	Unadjusted Trial Balance	
		Dr.	*Cr.*

NY

ber 31, 19--

justments	Adjusted Trial Balance		Income Statement		Balance Sheet	
Cr.	Dr.	Cr.	Dr.	Cr.	Dr.	Cr.

Name ______________________________

Section ______________ Date __________

1) and 2)

SHUSTER

Work

For the Year Ende

A/C #	Account	Deposits and Checks	
		Dr.	*Cr.*

r 30, 19X5

justments		Adjusted Trial Balance		Income Statement		Balance Sheet	
	Cr.	*Dr.*	*Cr.*	*Dr.*	*Cr.*	*Dr.*	*Cr.*

Name ____________________

Section ____________ Date __________

1. 1)

DUXAL CO

Work S

For the Year Ended Se

A/C #	Account	Unadjusted Trial Balance Dr.	Unadjusted Trial Balance Cr.
	Cash	8000	
	Accounts Receivable	25000	
	Merchandise Inventory	15000	
	Land	11000	
	Building	60000	
	Accumulated Depreciation–Building		22000
	Accounts Payable		12000
	Note Payable (long-term)		20000
	Francine Duxal, Capital		29000
	Francine Duxal, Withdrawals	5000	
	Sales		215000
	Sales Discounts	2000	
	Sales Returns and Allowances	3000	
	Rent Revenue		5000
	Purchases	130000	
	Purchases Discounts		1000
	Purchases Returns and Allowances		2000
	Transportation In	5000	
	Salaries Expense	35000	
	Advertising Expense	3000	
	Utilities Expense	4000	
		306000	306000

Name ______________________

Section ____________ Date ________

1)

FARKLEBE[R]

For the Mon[th]

A/C #	Account	Unadjusted Trial Balance Dr.	Unadjusted Trial Balance Cr.
11	Cash	2000	
12	Accounts Receivable	12000	
13	Fabrics Inventory	22000	
16	Equipment	6000	
016	Accumulated Depreciation–Equipment		2000
21	Accounts Payable		4600
25	Bank Loan Payable (due in 3 years)		8000
31	R. Nettles, Capital		20280
32	R. Nettles, Withdrawals	1000	
41	Sales		15000
42	Sales Returns and Allowances	800	
43	Sales Discounts Forfeited		160
51	Purchases	3000	
52	Purchases Returns and Allowances		200
53	Purchases Discounts Lost	50	
54	Freight In	100	
62	Salary Expense	2000	
63	Advertising Expense	510	
64	Utilities Expense	180	
65	Rent Expense	600	
		50240	50240
66	Depreciation Expense		
67	Interest Expense		
22	Interest Payable		
61	Cost of Goods Sold		

Adjustment Explanations

a) Depreciation for June.

b) Accrued Interest Payable at June 30.

PROBLEM 4.C.4. *(ALTERNATE ON REVERSE SIDE)*

ES

mber 31, 19--

Adjustments	Adjusted Trial Balance		Income Statement		Balance Sheet	
Cr.	Dr.	Cr.	Dr.	Cr.	Dr.	Cr.
b) 3000						
b) 2500						
a) 4800						

Name ____________________

Section ____________ Date ____________

1)

LEMEG

Worl

For the Year Ende

A/C #	Account	Unadjusted Trial Balance Dr.	Unadjusted Trial Balance Cr.	
111	Cash	18000		
112	Accounts Receivable	156000		
113	Merchandise Inventory	41000		
121	Furniture and Equipment	30000		
0121	Accumulated Depreciation–Furn. and Equip.		11000	
131	Land	15000		
141	Building	100000		
0141	Accumulated Depreciation–Building		12500	
211	Accounts Payable		18000	
221	Mortgage Payable (10 years)		49000	
311	W. Lemeg, Capital		116500	
312	W. Lemeg, Withdrawals	5000		
411	Sales		995000	
412	Sales Returns and Allowances	12000		
413	Rent Revenue		6000	
511	Purchases	580000		
512	Purchases Discounts		8000	
513	Purchases Returns and Allowances		5000	
514	Transportation In	14000		
612	Salaries Expense	210000		a)
613	Advertising Expense	21000		
614	Utilities Expense	16000		
615	Interest Expense	3000		
		1221000	1221000	
212	Salaries Payable			
616	Depreciation Expense			b)
611	Cost of Goods Sold			

Adjustment Explanations

a) Accrued salaries at year-end.

b) Depreciation for the year.

ABRICS STORE

heet

ed June 30, 19--

Adjustments		Adjusted Trial Balance		Income Statement		Balance Sheet	
Dr.	Cr.	Dr.	Cr.	Dr.	Cr.	Dr.	Cr.
	a) 600						
600							
40							
	b) 40						

justments		Adjusted Trial Balance		Income Statement		Balance Sheet	
	Cr.	Dr.	Cr.	Dr.	Cr.	Dr.	Cr.

Name ____________________

Section ____________ Date ____________

1)

____

Work

A/C #	Account	Unadjusted Trial Balance Dr.	Unadjusted Trial Balance Cr.
111	Cash		
112	Prepaid Insurance		
113	Accounts Receivable		
115	Merchandise Inventory		
116	Supplies		
118	Store Equipment		
0118	Accumulated Depreciation—Store Equipment		
211	Accounts Payable		
212	Notes Payable (due in 4 years)		
311	____________, Capital		
312	____________, Withdrawals		
411	Sales		
412	Sales Returns and Allowances		
413	Sales Discounts		
420	Rental Income		
512	Purchases		
513	Purchases Returns and Allowances		
514	Purchases Discounts		
515	Transportation In		
516	General Salaries Expense		
517	Advertising Expense		
518	Sales Salaries Expense		
519	Supplies Expense		
520	Depreciation Expense		
521	Rent Expense		
522	Insurance Expense		
511	Cost of Goods Sold		

(A)djustments		Adjusted Trial Balance		Income Statement		Balance Sheet	
	Cr.	*Dr.*	*Cr.*	*Dr.*	*Cr.*	*Dr.*	*Cr.*

Name ______________________________

Section ______________ Date ____________

1)

____

Work

A/C #	Account	Unadjusted Trial Balance	
		Dr.	Cr.
111	Cash		
112	Prepaid Insurance		
113	Accounts Receivable		
115	Merchandise Inventory		
116	Supplies		
118	Store Equipment		
0118	Accumulated Depreciation—Store Equipment		
211	Accounts Payable		
212	Notes Payable (due in 4 years)		
311	______________________, Capital		
312	______________________, Withdrawals		
411	Sales		
412	Sales Returns and Allowances		
413	Sales Discounts		
420	Rental Income		
512	Purchases		
513	Purchases Returns and Allowances		
514	Purchases Discounts		
515	Transportation In		
516	General Salaries Expense		
517	Advertising Expense		
518	Sales Salaries Expense		
519	Supplies Expense		
520	Depreciation Expense		
521	Rent Expense		
522	Insurance Expense		

ES

ber 31, 19--

justments		Adjusted Trial Balance		Income Statement		Balance Sheet	
	Cr.	Dr.	Cr.	Dr.	Cr.	Dr.	Cr.

Name ____________________

Section ____________ Date ____________

1)

O'CONNO

Work

For the Year Ende

A/C #	Account	Unadjusted Trial Balance Dr.	Unadjusted Trial Balance Cr.
	Cash	10000	
	Accounts Receivable	85000	
	Merchandise Inventory	180000	
	Store Fixtures	60000	
	Accumulated Depreciation		8000
	Accounts Payable		88000
	Bank Loan Payable		35000
	M. O'Connor, Capital		105000
	M. O'Connor, Withdrawals	20000	
	Sales		420000
	Purchases	185000	
	Wage Expense	80000	
	Rent Expense	24000	
	Other Expense	12000	
		656000	656000

djustments		Adjusted Trial Balance		Income Statement		Balance Sheet	
	Cr.	Dr.	Cr.	Dr.	Cr.	Dr.	Cr.

Name ______________________________

Section ______________ Date __________

3)

____

______________________ Wo

A/C #	Account	Unadjusted Trial Balance	
		Dr.	*Cr.*
111	Cash		
112	Accounts Receivable		
113	Merchandise Inventory		
116	Furnishings		
0116	Accumulated Depreciation–Furnishings		
211	Accounts Payable		
212	Wages Payable		
213	Notes Payable (due in 2 years)		
311	______________________, Capital		
312	______________________, Withdrawals		
411	Sales		
412	Sales Discounts		
413	Sales Returns and Allowances		
511	Purchases		
512	Purchases Discounts		
513	Purchases Returns and Allowances		
514	Transportation In		
611	Wage Expense		
612	Depreciation Expense		
613	Rent Expense		
510	Cost of Goods Sold		

...ustments		Adjusted Trial Balance		Income Statement		Balance Sheet	
	Cr.	Dr.	Cr.	Dr.	Cr.	Dr.	Cr.

Name ______________________________

Section ______________ Date ____________

3)

____

Work

____

A/C #	Account	Unadjusted Trial Balance	
		Dr.	*Cr.*
11	Cash		
12	Accounts Receivable		
13	Merchandise Inventory		
15	Furniture and Fixtures		
015	Accumulated Depreciation–Furniture and Fixtures		
21	Accounts Payable		
22	Salaries Payable		
23	Interest Payable		
24	Loan Payable (due in 3 years)		
31	______________________, Capital		
32	______________________, Withdrawals		
41	Sales		
42	Sales Discounts		
43	Sales Returns and Allowances		
52	Purchases		
53	Purchases Discounts		
54	Purchases Returns and Allowances		
55	Freight In		
61	Salary Expense		
62	Rent Expense		
63	Depreciation Expense		
64	Interest Expense		
51	Cost of Goods Sold		

NY

ril, 19--

justments	Adjusted Trial Balance		Income Statement		Balance Sheet	
Cr.	Dr.	Cr.	Dr.	Cr.	Dr.	Cr.

Name ____________

Section ________ Date ________

6)

CASE

Wor

For the Mon

A/C #	Account	Unadjusted Trial Balance Dr.	Cr.
111	Cash		
112	Accounts Receivable		
113	Merchandise Inventory		
116	Equipment		
0116	Accumulated Depreciation—Equipment		
211	Accounts Payable		
212	Sales Tax Payable		
215	Bank Loan Payable (due in 3 years)		
216	Interest Payable		
311	S. Case, Capital		
312	S. Case, Withdrawals		
411	Sales		
511	Purchases		
512	Freight In		
513	Purchases Discounts		
612	Wage Expense		
613	Rent Expense		
614	Advertising Expense		
615	Utilities Expense		
616	Depreciation Expense		
617	Interest Expense		
611	Cost of Goods Sold		

ANY

er 31, 19X4

ustments		Adjusted Trial Balance		Income Statement		Balance Sheet	
	Cr.	*Dr.*	*Cr.*	*Dr.*	*Cr.*	*Dr.*	*Cr.*

Name ____________________

Section ____________ Date __________

1)

R.H. MAY

Work

For the Year Ende

A/C #	Account	Unadjusted Trial Balance Dr.	Unadjusted Trial Balance Cr.
111	Cash	3000	
112	Prepaid Insurance	1800	
113	Accounts Receivable	12000	
0113	Allowance for Doubtful Accounts	30	
114	Note Receivable	2000	
116	Merchandise Inventory	22000	
121	Furniture and Equipment	22000	
0121	Accumulated Depreciation–Furn. and Equip.		1800
211	Accounts Payable		10800
215	Bank Loan Payable		8000
311	R.H. Mays, Capital		32260
312	R.H. Mays, Wihtdrawals	-0-	
411	Sales		170000
412	Sales Returns and Allowances	6000	
511	Purchases	111930	
512	Purchase Returns and Allowances		200
513	Freight In	500	
612	Salary Expense	31000	
613	Advertising Expense	5000	
614	Utilities Expense	1800	
615	Rent Expense	6000	
		223060	223060
616	Insurance Expense		
617	Depreciation Expense		
618	Interest Expense		
212	Interest Payabel		
619	Uncollectible Accounts Expense		
115	Interest Receivable		
413	Interest Revenue		
611	Cost of Good Sold		

[Ad]justments		Adjusted Trial Balance		Income Statement		Balance Sheet	
	Cr.	Dr.	Cr.	Dr.	Cr.	Dr.	Cr.

Name ______________________

Section ____________ Date ____________

____

Wo

____

A/C #	Account	Unadjusted Trial Balance	
		Dr.	Cr.
111	Cash		
112	Prepaid Insurance		
113	Prepaid Advertising		
115	Accounts Receivable		
0115	Allowance for Doubtful Accounts		
116	Merchandise Inventory		
118	Equipment		
0118	Accumulated Depreciation–Equipment		
211	Accounts Payable		
212	Bank Loan Payable		
213	Interest Payable		
311	______________, Capital		
312	______________, Withdrawals		
411	Sales		
412	Sales Returns and Allowances		
511	Purchases		
512	Purchases Discounts		
513	Purchases Returns and Allowances		
514	Freight In		
611	Salary Expense		
612	Rent Expense		
613	Insurance Expense		
614	Advertising Expense		
615	Utilities Expense		
616	Depreciation Expense		
617	Interest Expense		
618	Uncollectible Accounts Expense		
610	Cost of Goods Sold		

ustments	Adjusted Trial Balance		Income Statement		Balance Sheet	
Cr.	Dr.	Cr.	Dr.	Cr.	Dr.	Cr.

Name ______________________________

Section ______________ Date __________

1)

____

Wor

A/C #	Account	Unadjusted Trial Balance	
		Dr.	Cr.
	Cash		
	Accounts Receivable		
	Land		
	Machinery		
	Accumulated Depreciation—Machinery		
	Automotive Equipment		
	Accum. Depr.—Automotive Equipment		
	Building		
	Accumulated Depreciation—Building		
	Accounts Payable		
	Notes Payable (due 6/30/X5)		
	Mortgage Payable		
	______________________, Capital		
	Fees		
	Salary Expense		
	Utilities Expense		
	Supplies Expense		
	Interest Expense		
	Gasoline Expense		
	Other Expense		
	Depreciation Expense		

GISTER

*PAGE*________

rs e	Purchases	Freight In	Supplies	Salaries	Other Debits		
	Dr.	*Dr.*	*Dr.*	*Dr.*	*Account*	*Ref.*	*Amount*

Name ______________________

Section ____________ Date ____________

3. b.

VOUCH

Voucher No.	Date		Payee	Paid			
				Date		Ck. No.	

TER

PAGE ______

Purchases	Freight In	Supplies	Salaries	Other Debits		
				Account	*Ref.*	*Amount*
Dr.	*Dr.*	*Dr.*	*Dr.*			

Name ____________________

Section ______________ Date __________

2) and 3)

VOUCHE

Voucher No.	Date	Payee	Paid		V
			Date	Ck. No.	

STER

PAGE________

Purchases	Freight In	Supplies	Salaries	Other Debits		
Dr.	*Dr.*	*Dr.*	*Dr.*	*Account*	*Ref.*	*Amount*

Name ______________________

Section ____________ Date __________

2)

VOUCH

Voucher No.	Date		Payee	Paid Date		Paid Ck. No.	

TER

*PAGE*________

Purchases	Freight In	Supplies	Salaries	Other Debits		
Dr.	*Dr.*	*Dr.*	*Dr.*	*Account*	*Ref.*	*Amount*

Name ______________________

Section __________ Date __________

VOUCHE

Voucher No.	Date	Payee	Paid		V P
			Date	Ck. No.	

ISTER

*PAGE*________

s	Purchases	Freight In	Supplies	Salaries	Other Debits		
	Dr.	*Dr.*	*Dr.*	*Dr.*	*Account*	*Ref.*	*Amount*

Name ______________________________

Section ______________ Date ___________

VOUCHE

Voucher No.	Date	Payee	Paid		V
			Date	*Ck. No.*